FIT
TO BE
A
PASTOR

Other Books by G. Lloyd Rediger

Coping with Clergy Burnout

Lord, Don't Let Me Be Bored

Ministry and Sexuality: Cases, Counseling, and Care

*Clergy Killers: Guidance for Pastors
and Congregations under Attack*

FIT

TO BE

A

PASTOR

A Call to Physical, Mental, and Spiritual Fitness

G. Lloyd Rediger

Westminster John Knox Press
Louisville, Kentucky

Scripture quotations from the New Revised Standard Version of the Bible are copyright © 1989 by the Division of Christian Education of the National Council of the Churches of Christ in the U.S.A. and are used by permission.

Book design by Sharon Adams
Cover design by PAZ Design Group

First edition
Published by Westminster John Knox Press
Louisville, Kentucky

This book is printed on acid-free paper that meets the American National Standards Institute Z39.48 standard. ♾

PRINTED IN THE UNITED STATES OF AMERICA

00 01 02 03 04 05 06 07 08 09 — 10 9 8 7 6 5 4 3 2 1

Library of Congress Cataloging-in-Publication Data
Rediger, G. Lloyd.
    Fit to be a pastor : a call to physical, mental, and spiritual
fitness / G. Lloyd Rediger.—1st ed.
        p. cm.
    Includes bibliographical references.
    ISBN 0-664-25844-1 (alk. paper)
    1. Clergy—Health and hygiene. I. Title.

BV4397.5 .R43 1999
248.8′92—dc21   99-045357

*To pastors already dedicated to
and participating in a fitness quest*

CONTENTS

ACKNOWLEDGMENTS

Though I have been on my own fitness quest for some years, I am still learning its intricacies, benefits, and possibilities. I am grateful to spiritual leaders, researchers, and writers in the disciplines of health, spirituality, and fitness whose insights have inspired and guided me. With deep appreciation I acknowledge support and guidance from these spiritual leaders: Robert Bohl, David Owen, David Brown, Roger Cantril, Doug Kelly, Bruce Hartung, Ron Weinelt, Larry Collins, and Jeanne Maruska.

I acknowledge and value the guidance I have received from my editor, Stephanie Egnotovich. She has shared her insights and experience without reserve, and been both critical and supportive in ways only a fine editor can be. Tom Maiuro has supported and guided my enthusiasm for getting the message of fitness to clergy in special ways only a fine publicist and marketing specialist can provide. I am pleased to be published again by Westminster John Knox Press.

Vera Hansen Rediger is my esteemed partner, not only in producing the manuscript for this book, but through countless conversations about the realities of human life and spiritual leadership. There is no one whose life and insights I respect more. I also acknowledge the support of our son, Richard Lloyd Hansen, and daughter-in-law, Heather Ann Hansen, for listening patiently and thoughtfully as I tested ideas. The physical, mental, and spiritual fitness of my family inspires me continually.

Finally, I acknowledge a great debt to organized religion and the Presbyterian Church (U.S.A.). For the church is the milieu in which I learned, practiced, and now share my understanding of effective spiritual leadership. And I am thankful continually to God for life, health, and discernment in my personal fitness quest.

INTRODUCTION

Life is possible . . . Jesus Christ said that he had come so that we could live our lives to the fullest (John 10:10b). Yet for many Americans "life to the fullest" is only a vague daily possibility. We tend to live between stress and pleasure, hoping that something worthwhile will happen. Though our economy is flourishing and America is the "land of plenty" and "the good life," there is little inner peace, little security, little joy. The evidence is our endemic unfitness of body, mind, and spirit. We try to cope rather than to learn fitness. Worst of all, our unfitness is so common that we think it is normal—we don't even realize how unfit (unhealthy) we are, nor the detrimental consequences.

We know we can do better than this. So we struggle on, trying this, buying that, and imagining that somehow it will all turn out to give us the life we always hoped for. This book is about one of those struggles—a struggle to live a healthy, fit life. The struggle, however, is unnecessary and counterproductive. When we pause and understand what Jesus meant by living life to its fullest, we can find out what health really is. It is body-mind-spirit fitness. Our struggle then becomes a quest.

Fitness is a hot subject—but apparently not hot enough. According to recent news reports, statistics indicate that despite publicized efforts of government, medical, and mental health agencies, our fitness is not improving. And we still lead the world in the incidence of life-threatening and disabling diseases. The good news about the enormous benefits of fitness is not getting through.

Fitness is not a hot subject in organized religion . . . *yet!* True, we have a few more parish nurse programs and a few more ministers of counseling, but we have few concerted efforts to raise the health and fitness levels of congregations and spiritual leaders. Our ministries tend to be oriented toward Band-Aids rather than full health. Moreover, clergy exhibit the same symptoms of unfitness that most parishioners do. Our endemic clergy version of unfitness is marked by stress, depression, and role confusion. We can do better than this.

This book is about the new/old gospel of fitness. Body-mind-spirit fitness, which I sometimes refer to as BMS fitness, is for pastors, for congregations, for our nation, and for the "geofamily." Such fitness is a blend of biblical wholeness, the healing-health model of Jesus Christ, and the latest insights of many professionals in bodily fitness, mental fitness, and spiritual fitness. It is apparent that being fit in only body, mind, or spirit is not truly fitness. The "fullness-of-life" fitness Jesus promised occurs when body, mind, and spirit are fit—together. Such a rich experience of life is worthy of considerable attention.

A popularized version of fitness is distracting us from the realities of body-mind-spirit fitness. Ads for pills, diet fads, and exercise gimmicks have convinced us that fitness can be achieved by buying something, paying a physician to fix us, or trying something new. The realities of fitness, however, are three: it is simple, we must do it ourselves, and it must include body, mind, and spirit.

A further distraction from reality is the glamour and performance paradigm that attracts or repels us with illusory images of muscles, physical beauty, and marathon-type endurance. BMS fitness, on the other hand, is realistic. It is for each and all of us, with our idiosyncrasies, limits, and potentials, and with our shared needs and resources. This fitness is not perfection—it is about being the best that you can be, as you are and can become. It is a choice between fitness and unfitness. It is an attitude in which you see fitness as a joyful, energized pilgrimage, rather than a drudgery devoid of pleasure, peace, and success. It is a satisfying discipline that leads us into God's purposes for us, for the community of faith, and for all of creation. Fitness is good stewardship. And this is your—our—fitness quest.

The benefits of body-mind-spirit fitness are enormous: fitness feels better, looks better, works better, plays better, relates better—and it costs less. But fitness is not automatic. Discipline is required, as in achieving anything worthwhile. A fresh, realistic vision of what fitness is leads to a decision to become the best that you can be, which in turn leads to developing a lifestyle that produces and sustains BMS fitness. Fitness becomes its own reward.

Though this book emphasizes individual fitness, it can be a model for body-mind-spirit fitness in congregations. Since communities of faith are organic entities ("You are the body of Christ," 1 Cor. 12:27; Eph. 5:30), they function with the same dynamics that an individual experiences in body, mind, and spirit. When a congregation begins to understand itself the body-mind-spirit of Jesus Christ reincarnated, it will develop its own shared BMS fitness quest. And it will experience the enormous benefits an individual experiences. It should be apparent that the endemic unfitness found in so many congregations (exhibited in conflict, abuse of pastors, spiritual malaise, degeneration, and decline) will be lessened, and spiritual vigor will be generated when we all seek fitness instead of indulgence. Being the best that we can be—together—is an empowering vision for any congregation. BMS fitness is for all of us.

This book is a primer on fitness: body-mind-spirit fitness. As a primer it provides a starting place and a review of relevant information and possibilities. It remains for each of us to write the full textbook of our own BMS fitness. Even if we know about fitness, continual review and assessment are required for our contemporary society, which distracts us with ephemeral pleasures of unfitness. We get sick when we forget how to be well. BMS fitness must become a counterculture. We can no longer afford the distractions of a culture that is giving itself to consumerism, indulgence, and incivility if we want to be healthy ourselves and be effective witnesses to the gospel of Jesus Christ. Our society is not all bad, of course. We need not destroy or vilify it, for it is still the finest nation on earth to most of us. Yet it is becoming morally and spiritually and physically sick unto death. And because the church now reflects society instead of leading it, we must again separate ourselves from the symptoms and causes of a sickness I am here calling unfitness. Then we can recover the insights and mission of God's purposes.

Some pastors have found the secret of fitness, but many have not. Clergy unfitness is a shared as well as a personal problem and responsibility. Our unfit lifestyles can be hidden easily in the mystique, roles, and rituals of pastoring. And since we have now convinced ourselves and parishioners that we have a right to be like everyone else, there is less expectation that we will model and teach anything more than what people are already doing. We will need an attitude of confession and repentance for this malfeasance. We will need healing from our spiritual, mental, and physical sicknesses. And we will need to reinvent a healthy pastoral role based upon body-mind-spirit fitness if we are to honor God's call to faithful stewardship of our personhood and devotion to God's purposes. For the health and fitness of clergy is crucial to the health and fitness of the church. And who is a more appropriate leader in the crusade for BMS fitness than a fit pastor? Surgeon General David Satcher has stated publicly that he believes clergy should be in the forefront of this crusade even as they were in the early civil rights movement. This fits our calling.

Thank God that health is as contagious as sickness. As I travel across the United States and do seminars and retreats on spiritual leadership issues, I see a beginning of fresh spiritual insights and recovery of our God-given mission. Much of this is based upon elements of body-mind-spirit fitness. In this book I attempt to recognize and distill these reassuring developments. When a pastor and a community of faith get a taste of BMS fitness, sickness is engulfed in health, and God's purposes in our midst tend to unify and energize us.

I begin in chapter 1 with case studies of unfitness in pastors and explain how they found fitness or turned away from it. These are cases from my own experience as a pastor and as a pastoral counselor to clergy and their families. The first chapter also includes some clergy fitness quizzes that will enable you to focus and personalize the body-mind-spirit perspective on unfitness and fitness. Following the cases and quizzes are some common questions and answers about the fitness quest.

In chapter 2, I explore the context of contemporary unfitness in our society and church. Statistics indicate the dire state of our nation's health, and the alarming costs and consequences of indulgent consumerism and an attitude of entitlement. The community of faith similarly contains distractions, role confusions, and vulnerabilities that seduce or confuse unfit pastors and laity. Then I return to my earlier questions regarding the motivations of clergy and congregations for fitness in the national, local, and personal contexts just discussed. Two concepts important for our motivation toward body-mind-spirit fitness are introduced. One is "adventure," an attitude of exciting curiosity, openness, and discovery that appears as the new satisfactions of fitness replace the seeming comforts of unfitness. The other is "disintermediation," the act of disengaging from unhealthy codependencies and taking responsibility for our own BMS fitness. Both of these help people break the inertia that tends to imprison us in habitual unfitness.

In chapter 3, I define terms and present the ABCs of body-mind-spirit fitness. This gives an opportunity for us to think through the information and misinformation attached to our assumptions about health, wellness, wholeness, spirituality, and fitness.

Healing is the theme of chapter 4. This may seem to be an unusual aspect of fitness, but full fitness cannot be achieved without healing, for all of us need to be healed from something, and for something. Love, which we all value as the goal of our faith, is not possible in a state of unfitness, except in distorted forms. Religion tends to use the word "love" as if it were a panacea or something we just decide to do. But the love that Jesus lived and taught is a function of body-mind-spirit fitness, rather than the producer of it. When we are fully fit, love will be as normal as breathing.

In chapter 5, I begin to explore the three components of body-mind-spirit fitness. Bodily fitness is the focus, but I note mental and spiritual connections. The mental component of BMS fitness is the theme of chapter 6, and in chapter 7, I discuss spiritual fitness. In chapter 8, BMS fitness is presented as fulfillment—of our deepest needs, motivations, and potentials. And chapter 9 applies the ABCs of fitness to congregations. This chapter notes that the community of faith is a living organism called the body of Christ in the New Testament. Therefore the fitness ABCs laid out in this book are applicable for a congregation. An outline of a curriculum for teaching fitness in congregations is offered.

The final chapter is a call for a national, ecumenical clergy fitness initiative. The growing wave of health/fitness consciousness in North America is noted as a God-given opportunity for the church to help shape all this awareness into spiritual and mental and physical health. So I issue an urgent plea for pastors to lead in this movement. For spiritual health is crucial in body-mind-spirit fitness.

The appendixes provide three resources for body-mind-spirit fitness. One is a systematic three-year plan for the development of clergy fitness. This plan includes a suggested daily fitness regimen. It allows for individual needs and possibilities. And it recommends movement toward interpersonal relationships that will support growth and hold participants accountable for personal and professional development. Another resource is a fitness worksheet for organizing life history and potential for fitness. Yet another is the Body-Mind-Spirit-Fitness Regimen Outline, which summarizes a daily-weekly regimen.

A bibliography is provided, with annotations for books deemed especially significant for the clergy fitness quest.

This book is not a solution for all that ails us. Yet it is offered with a sincere prayer that fit clergy and fit congregations shall once again lead the way into the new and rewarding possibilities that are called body-mind-spirit fitness in this book. Along with medical and mental health professionals we can become a potent team for fitness in a time when the consequences of unfitness threaten to engulf the geofamily. Thank God, health is as contagious as sickness.

May God help us to see, hear, and experience body-mind-spirit fitness as a joyous part of our salvation, and as a prescription for the spiritual illnesses that divide us.

1

Are You Fit to Be a Pastor?

> We get sick when we
> forget how to be well.
> *Anonymous*

THREE FITNESS CASES

Life is possible . . . but each of us must live it in our own way. Stories from real life help us to explore other possible lifestyles. I begin with the stories of three real people, all pastors struggling to understand and live body-mind-spirit fitness.

Cal Hopkins was doing fine. He was very busy, as successful or effective pastors are expected to be these days. His growing congregation of several hundred members was located in a small town near a major metropolitan area. The church building was historic and located on a scenic river. Many professionals and laborers who worked in the city but preferred small-town ambiance lived within driving distance of Cal's church. The congregation had developed an intense style, with many programs and small study-support groups. There were normal conflicts and antagonisms, yet the congregation absorbed these into its stimulating and creative attitude.

Cal was gregarious, competent, and active in all phases of the congregation's life, and that of the community. He traveled into the city often to make hospital calls and attend study events. He and his wife, Betty Ann, had three children in lower grade and middle schools. She was a professional financial advisor working part-time for a prominent investment firm.

I learned of Cal's secret life only after several informal lunches we shared. We met at a seminar I did for area clergy, and he asked if we could have lunch. At our first lunch it was apparent that he wanted to cite his successes. By the end of our conversation it was also apparent that, beneath the jovial exterior, he was troubled. He asked to set another lunch date. I countered by suggesting that we make an appointment to meet at my pastoral counseling office. His reluctance led to another lunch meeting. This time his anxieties were apparent from the beginning. He apologized for his weight, ordering cocktails, the handful of pills he took after lunch, and taking so much of my time. To postpone effusive revelations for a more appropriate setting, I asked some general questions, and then referred to the seminar he had attended where I discussed unfitness among pastors and some generic remedies. As we finished, I again suggested an appointment, but he insisted on meeting at this restaurant again. Realizing the importance of this process to him, I agreed. He always picked up the meal check.

At our next lunch he arrived early and arranged for us to sit in a secluded area of the restaurant. As soon as I sat down he poured out a story of growing awareness that in spite of his professional achievements, his personal life was deteriorating in serious ways. He was overeating to compensate for anxious guilt feelings, drinking more alcohol to assuage his suspicions about rumors in the congregation, and becoming so busy with church work that he could no longer prepare appropriately for his sermons and classes. When he was at home, he was spending more time watching TV and falling asleep in his recliner. The children were at home less, and Betty Ann was distancing herself from him. The secret part was his continuing indulgence in pornography, compulsive masturbation, and occasional visits to a sexual massage parlor. He had become infatuated with a woman in the congregation with whom he often worked on congregational projects. It was his fantasizing about her sexually, to the point where he considered inviting her to travel to a church conference with him, that finally forced him to break through his denials of how unfit he had become. For he realized that such an assignation would likely result in disaster.

After listening to his anguished confession, I acknowledged his pain and the dangers in his lifestyle. And he acknowledged the realities I shared with him, that a thorough transformation of his lifestyle was needed. Now he was ready to visit me in the office. It was reassuring, in our office appointments, to see his ego strength, his healthy fear of what was happening, and his ready acceptance of the prescriptions we developed for physical-mental-spiritual recovery and fitness. One of the prescriptions was for his marriage and family and required the involvement of Betty Ann and his children.

Cal had caught himself before most of the disastrous consequences of his overeating, drinking, and escapism caught up with him. He has since chosen health and fitness instead of self-destruction.

I hear from him through his Christmas letter each year now. The family picture on the letter, and his handwritten note on the back of each letter indicate that he is enjoying a life of disciplined and reassuring fitness.

Rachel Edwards was in her second pastorate. It was a bucolic setting with a yoked parish of two small churches in neighboring towns. She was single and in her second vocation, after leaving grade school teaching in frustration at the deterioration of public education. She had been disappointed with her first appointment to a small, troubled congregation, so the bishop had honored her request for a move by offering the present appointment. There had seemed to be no alternative, so she accepted it about two years ago. Now she was feeling frustration similar to that which had ended her teaching career. A deep anger had developed, and she had someone she could blame—several, in fact. The bishop, her district superintendent, and her clergy colleagues were on the list, with some hints that God would soon be there as well. In her growing depression, she was even blaming herself for colluding in the decline of her career, and she hated being a woman and single.

I learned of Rachel's misery in our first pastoral counseling appointment. We quickly settled into a weekly appointment pattern in which she vented her anger for the early part of the appointment, and then quite obviously sank into a morose embodiment of her despair. Her need for biochemical support was apparent, so I referred her to my psychiatric consultant. These were the halcyon days of Prozac's portentous emergence, and her mood improved rather quickly. But the cognitive pattern and lifestyle remained the same. When the psychiatrist required a thorough physical exam, some deeper maladies became apparent. And during her lifestyle review, admitting her lack of mental nurture and physical exercise brought tears to her eyes. She hadn't attended a concert or serious theater or visited an art museum since her days as a teacher. And she no longer had her racquetball club and friends as exercise partners. There were no such facilities anywhere near where she presently lived. Further, her meditational exercises had become routine and boring.

Rachel was functioning at what appeared to be a normal level. She did the usual preaching, hospital calls, and communions, and she taught a Bible study class and attended most committee meetings. But there was no inspiration in her pastoral services and little growth in her spiritual life. Her mind was becoming undisciplined, her spirit depressed, and her body flabby. And there was no outside moral support or incentive for change and improvement.

I asked Rachel to share responsibility for her healing and recovery, and for a fitness quest. I asked her to start by selecting a pastoral counseling method that she felt would be most supportive to her healing, recovery, and fitness quest. The options were: continue in the cognitive mode we were in, with medical assistance; co-counseling with a female counselor; or move into a spiritual director mode. She thought and prayed about these options between appointments. When she came the next time, she was decisive in choosing spiritual direction. I reviewed again the basic process of spiritual direction, then we went into a time of silent reflection in which I suggested that she develop a mental picture of Jesus healing the woman suffering from hemorrhages as if this were her own healing. We read the Mark 5:25–34 story in unison before becoming silent. Not long into the silence she reached for the box of tissues and then began to sob quietly. Soon her crying became deep, wrenching sobs accompanied by tight-fisted pounding on the arms of her chair. After a time, the sobs metamorphosed into a soft whimpering, then into a pleading prayer, "Jesus, please heal me!" A period of silent crying followed, and then a soft repetition of the words, "Jesus Christ, I accept my healing, and thank you for my new life."

After reviewing this healing process in the next appointment, I discussed the principles of wholeness with her. Then I suggested that she begin keeping a regular journal of her spiritual fitness quest. In the next appointment, after our meditation-reflection time, I asked Rachel if her journal entries were indicating whether her body, mind, or spirit was dominant in her experience of wholeness thus far. She replied that her spirit was dominating her consciousness in the entries. She told of how a feeling of deep thankfulness had emerged briefly, but was quickly blocked by a sense of betrayal, desertion, injustice, and aloneness, accompanied by anger. When I asked what she believed was the spiritual prescription for such feelings, she thought for a long time, then answered with a wry smile, "Forgiveness." This became an opportunity, in the next several appointments, to explore the steps of the forgiveness formula. (Note: The forgiveness formula and wholeness will be discussed more fully in chapter 4.) Her feelings of thankfulness returned, and from thankfulness emerged a fresh sense of her call to parish ministry. She journaled and found profound stimulation in the biblical stories of women in ministry. Next came an exploration of the stewardship of her spiritual-mental-physical "gifts and graces." Rachel was becoming excited about her pastoral ministries again.

Her rejuvenated spirit, however, could not overcome the physical malady that was sapping her energy. Her psychiatrist referred Rachel for a diagnostic exam, and an internist finally diagnosed her condition as lupus. A series of medicating efforts followed, with mixed success. Her physical condition deteriorated until she was unable to drive her car. Even with all the medications, she became more depressed about her condition. The bishop recommended a six-month leave of absence. During this time she underwent an intensive medical regimen and applied for Social Security SSI benefits. With supplemental financial aid she purchased an electric convenience vehicle. This portable battery-powered scooter allowed her to navigate with less drain on physical energy. A friend in the community was engaged to act as her car driver.

The leave of absence allowed physicians to stabilize her condition. Our counseling appointments continued. Shortly after her return to pastoral duties, the thought of physical healing emerged in our prayers and reflections. We planned a healing service for a Sunday afternoon in her church. Her bishop and I led a liturgical service, with most of her parishioners and several relatives and close friends in attendance. It was a deeply moving service. Yet there was no evidence of increasing mobility, mood elevation, or invigoration.

In our next appointment, we reviewed the healing service in a meditative-reflective mode. Following a long period of silence, she noted that the healing hadn't produced what she most wanted—physical healing. But, she noted, mental-spiritual healing had occurred. She believed that she could now incorporate her physical limitations into her fitness quest.

Over several months Rachel and I followed the mental images that emerged in our meditation-reflection periods and her journal entries. I added anecdotes of healthy ministry and self-care. Her explorations came to include a competent nutrition-fasting, exercise-resting, work-recreation regimen, in which her body was invigorated and strengthened in modest ways. We related what she was learning from the physical regimen to her mental and spiritual patterns. These were then translated into a schedule that included pastoral ministries and self-care. By this time she had revived several old friendships and developed a local support system.

When I asked her if there were key factors in her transformation, she thought for a while. Then she responded, "I think my attitude had to change first. I saw this attitude I had developed, and didn't like what I saw. Then, I had to reassess my beliefs—what I really believed about God, the church, my life. I had become cynical about the beliefs I professed. And finally, I saw what an empty, unhealthy lifestyle I had developed without realizing it. The healing service was a major turning point. For in that healing process I came to terms with my limitations. I had to change my mental image of myself to include a physically limited person who was still called to be a pastor. It has been difficult to build a fitness lifestyle, but now the results have convinced me that this is the only way to live and do ministry."

Her parishioners noticed and affirmed her healing and growth. Her bishop heard the reports, and within a year he offered her a more stimulating appointment. She requested instead that the bishop reappoint her to the present yoked parish, and support her teaching and writing efforts to share her good news about the fitness quest. Some years later, she is now a district superintendent and a mentor to other pastors.

John Jenkins never quite made it—he still hasn't. He's in his mid-thirties, has six children, and is married to Sarah, a childhood sweetheart who is a laid-back, self-employed artist. John did well in college as a social studies major, then had an adequate academic record in seminary. He is rather shy, in a pleasant way, yet is competent in social settings. Not very active physically, he likes to putter around the house, play with his kids, and watch TV. He has been putting on weight over the years and dresses very casually. His lifestyle and pastoring style have become more easygoing, which fit Sarah's laid-back manner.

John's easygoing style and appearance belie an inner turmoil. I learned this in our first pastoral counseling appointment. In fact, his opening statement was, "I know that I look relaxed and casual, but I'm not. Inside I'm unhappy most of the time. I would call myself lazy and even slovenly. It's the story of my life. The only time I started to pull myself together was when I left home and began to do rather well in my college studies. Then I got married and we immediately began to have kids. I had admired my pastor, so I thought I'd try going into the ministry. But in seminary I started to slide back into the lazy lifestyle I grew up in. We were all like that. Now here I am in my third pastorate and not sure if I can ever be anything more than a barely competent pastor. My little churches have accepted me pretty much as I am, but I don't like what I am."

He was silent for a while, and I was reviewing in my mind this rehearsed and unhappy summary of his life and ministry. Without prompting, John soon resumed his story by telling of attempts he had made to improve himself. At one point he said, "I am very good at making New Year's resolutions. In fact this is one of the ways I torture myself. Just recently I took a continuing education course in preaching and came home from it determined to establish good study and preparation habits in order to improve my preaching. But here I am, a month later, back in the same old rut."

After another period of silence, he stared at me and then said, "What do you think of my story?" I replied, "Well, you haven't told me yet that your lifestyle and self-image are getting worse and worse, and that it is hopeless to try and improve yourself."

"And I thought you were going to be my friend," he replied, with a pained smile.

"That's interesting," I said. "But I think you came here for more than that."

In our next appointment I asked him to stand in front of the full-length mirror in my office. This generated wry jokes about physical appearance and considerable discomfort. I asked him not to turn away or use his usual coping strategies, but rather to just look—until he could give an accurate assessment of what and who he was. This process continued over a couple more appointments, accompanied by journaling about his life at home. We invited Sarah to join us for one session. But it was quickly apparent that she was not comfortable talking of change or of participating in John's fitness quest.

John and I agreed to a long-term psychotherapy program. He cooperated easily and seemed to enjoy reviewing his earlier years in-depth and compiling a family history. As we devised some growth and change strategies, however, his resistance became apparent. He wanted to try a change in preaching preparation again, but though the effort started well, the outcome was familiar—he stopped. I suggested that we do something more basic. So we embarked on a physical-mental-spiritual fitness exploration and regimen, beginning with an effort to improve nutrition and exercise patterns. He was mildly enthusiastic for several weeks. Then, although he had never mentioned that he planned a career move, he announced that he had accepted a call from a small but well-established congregation in a town near the place where he spent his childhood years and where his mother and siblings still lived.

In a couple of weeks he and his family had moved. In our last appointment he thanked me and said, "I appreciate your efforts, but I guess I really don't want to change."

THE PERSONAL CONTEXT OF FITNESS

My personal experience with body-mind-spirit fitness is checkered. My early models were pastors, some of whom were exemplary. As I grew, I revered explorers and athletes. When my education introduced me to great thinkers, they became my models. Most recently I appreciate leaders in theology, mental health, social justice, and the arts. Having seen some of these persons up close, I no longer idealize them. But the ones I respect the most are the ones with personal integrity, dedication, and moral-spiritual discipline—body-mind-spirit fitness.

I, too, have flaws, disabilities, and limitations. I sometimes struggle with my personal fitness regimen. Many of the lessons I have learned about body-mind-spirit fitness have come the hard way; others have been learned through success. And I am thankful to God, intimates, mentors, and organized religion for the privileges I have had in developing BMS fitness in my personal life, as well as assisting others on this pilgrimage. This book is based upon such human experiences.

These three cases and my personal experience do not exhaust all perspectives on the quest for fitness in pastoral ministry. They do, however, provide a recognizable context as we explore the value of physical-mental-spiritual fitness. The above cases show three pastors. One recognizes his unfitness, seeks help, and develops an appropriate body-mind-spirit fitness regimen and lifestyle. The second pastor has trouble recognizing her personal unfitness, which becomes complicated by physical disability, yet perseveres to find a BMS fitness regimen and lifestyle appropriate for her. The third pastor vaguely senses unfitness, makes sporadic efforts toward fitness, but finally turns back to his normal unfitness.

Now you will need to think through your own life story, for it is the most relevant context for understanding and developing your personal fitness quest. You can begin with a personal assessment: are you fit or unfit to be a pastor today?

Answering the questions on the fitness quizzes that follow is a simple way to focus on the vulnerabilities of unfitness, and thereby write ourselves a prescription for personal and pastoral health. This inventory is presented in two forms, one to help highlight unfitness and the other to highlight fitness. The two versions are intended to minimize bias in the wording of the inventories and to help you notice how you think about your personal and professional fitness or unfitness. Seeing personal data gets our attention, even if the data are informal. These versions of the inventory introduce significant issues in the personal and professional lives of pastors. Answer both sets of questions.

PASTORAL UNFITNESS QUIZ

Underline one response in answer to the following questions.

1. Do you avoid regular, vigorous exercise? (yes or no)
2. Do you frequently worry about not being a good pastor? (yes or no)
3. Do you avoid attending artistic events? (yes or no)
4. Do you take antacids more than once a month? (yes or no)
5. Do you distrust most of your parishioners? (yes or no)
6. Do you feel unloved? (yes or no)
7. Are you more than ten pounds overweight? (yes or no)
8. Do you avoid taking at least one day off per week? (yes or no)
9. Do you frequently want to leave pastoral ministry? (yes or no)
10. Do you often feel exhausted before noon? (yes or no)
11. Do you frequently have trouble making decisions? (yes or no)
12. Do you often feel bored with your meditative practices? (yes or no)
13. Do you get sick frequently? (yes or no)

Total yes answers _____ Total no answers _____

Now go back and reread these questions and think again about your answers without changing them. What do you feel? Do not second-guess your responses, for your first reaction is what is wanted here.

Scoring. You know how such quizzes are scored from seeing similar ones in popular magazines. For this one, if you answered yes to all ten, "seek help!" Answering yes to seven or more is a serious indicator that you have need of immediate, healthful remedies. If you answered yes to five or more, you are on the borderline of serious dysfunction as a pastor. If you answered yes to three or less, you are probably normally neurotic and occasionally malfunctional. These proportions are based on commonsense recognition that the more troubling issues there are in your life, the more likelihood there is of vulnerability and dysfunction. If you answered yes to questions 5, 6, 9, and 10, I encourage you to consult a certified pastoral counselor or spiritual director, or a mental health professional who takes religious faith seriously. For these represent troubling issues for pastors.

This is not a scientifically rigorous test, of course. But it certainly will give you some indicators about your fitness to be a pastor. You will notice that these questions probe the physical and mental and spiritual aspects of fitness. Though they are very general, each question examines a cluster of unhealthy characteristics that are common to unfit clergy. And though a particular question may not touch a sensitive issue for you, it likely touches a troubling cluster of issues that concern you at times. For these are factors that appear regularly in my counseling of pastors.

Answering yes to any of these questions does not make you unfit to be a pastor. But each question suggests again how common our unfitness has become. If you answered no to most questions, take a moment to consider why you answered no.

Pastoral Fitness Quiz

The first quiz approached the fitness-unfitness process by focusing on unfitness. Now, below, a similar quiz focuses on positive fitness. As you answer these questions, reframed, you may experience a bifocal or holographic perspective. This can induce a stimulating comparison.

Underline one response in answer to the following questions.

1. Do you participate in regular, vigorous exercise? (yes or no)
2. Do you believe that you are a good pastor? (yes or no)
3. Do you attend artistic events regularly? (yes or no)
4. Do you use antacids less than once per month? (yes or no)
5. Do you trust nearly all of your parishioners? (yes or no)
6. Do you almost always feel loved? (yes or no)
7. Do you maintain a weight normal for your age, height, gender? (yes or no)
8. Do you consistently take at least one day off per week? (yes or no)
9. Do you seldom think of leaving pastoral ministry? (yes or no)

10. Do you feel normally energetic all day long? (yes or no)
11. Do you nearly always make decisions easily? (yes or no)
12. Do you consistently feel satisfied by your meditational exercises? (yes or no)
13. Do you seldom get sick? (yes or no)

Total yes answers_____ Total no answers_____

Now go back and reread these questions and think again about your answers without changing them. What responses do you feel? Do not second-guess your responses, for your first reaction is what is wanted here.

Scoring. For this one, if you answered no to all thirteen, "seek help!" If you answered yes to seven or more, you should take a serious look at those to which you answered no. For they likely show a concentration of fitness in bodily, mental, or spiritual areas. If you answered yes to ten or more, you likely are functioning adequately. If you answered yes to all thirteen, you are functioning beyond normal expectations and may be deluding yourself. In such a case, either be very thankful or review your capacity for insight.

Again, this is not a scientifically rigorous test, but it will give you some indicators about your fitness to be a pastor. The questions touch on the physical, mental, and spiritual aspects of fitness. Though they are general, each question indicates a cluster of health characteristics that are common to fit clergy. And though a particular question may not touch a sensitive issue for you, it likely touches a cluster of issues you have thought about at times. For these are factors that appear regularly in the counseling of pastors.

Answering yes to these questions does not make you fit to be a pastor, nor does answering no to most of them mean you are unfit. But thinking and praying about these issues may encourage you to review your physical-mental-spiritual health and fitness.

Now compare your responses to both quizzes. Did you find yourself in the case studies? What influence did they have on your responses?

PERSPECTIVE

One of the slogans we have heard in recent years is "Be all that you can be" (as in the U.S. Army recruiting slogan).

The goal and motivation in this slogan fits for all Americans, young and old, no matter their social class, ethnic heritage, or gender. And it is good stewardship of body-mind-spirit. This slogan calls to clergy in some unique ways, for myriad distractions, vulnerabilities, and abuses hinder our efforts to be the best we can be, leaving us in danger of becoming unfit to be pastors.

The remedy is to first recover our physical, mental, and spiritual health. Second, we can put those distractions, vulnerabilities, and abuses into proper perspective. And third, we can move ourselves and our parishioners toward the worthy goal of being the best that we can be—under God, and for God's purposes.

There are two keys to this contemporary reformation among pastors. One is *fitness:* "being the best that we can be." The second is *attitude:* "Pastoring—the toughest job you'll ever love" (as in the Peace Corps motto). This attitudinal love is tough love, not ingratiating love. These keys are prominent in this book.

Gaining a clearer understanding of your personal fitness, as a person and as a pastor, is a good place to start. But we will then move on to an understanding that fitness is also important for our pastoral ministry, our parishioners, our denomination, our nation.

In the clinical sense, fitness is disciplined self-management. In the spiritual sense, fitness is blending with God's purposes. In the everyday, physical meaning, fitness is the practice of wellness. The way to be the best that we can be is to nourish and exercise our bodies, minds, and spirits in ways appropriate to their needs and functions, rather than in service to our appetites, habits, and anxieties. Fitness is not only a good idea and good theology, it is doable.

ASK YOURSELF SOME QUESTIONS

The answers to the following questions point toward general positive responses that will help initiate a fitness quest.

WHY SHOULD I BE INTERESTED IN FITNESS?

Fitness is its own reward—the benefits are enormous:

Fitness feels better.
Fitness looks better.
Fitness works better.
Fitness plays better.
Fitness relates better.
   And . . . fitness costs less!

A majority of Americans are overweight, exercise too little, and have unhealthy lifestyles, as documented by reports from medical professionals, mental health professionals, and polling data (statistics from National Center for Health Statistics, American Heart Association, National Institutes of Health). Our most worrisome indicator of unfitness, however, is our entitlement attitude, by which I mean that we have come to believe that we have a right to be as unfit as we want, no matter the costs and consequences. Health care now costs us a trillion dollars per year . . . most of it unnecessary. And even with the most advanced medical resources in the world, Americans have the highest incidence of serious illnesses—heart disease, cancer, diabetes—of any nation. We cannot afford these consequences of indulgent lifestyles much longer. Thank God there seems to be a growing awareness that health and fitness are the prescription for many of our personal and social illnesses. And health and fitness are now being seen as a personal and shared responsibility.

WHY SHOULD THE CHURCH BE CONCERNED ABOUT FITNESS?

There is no other institution better positioned spiritually and logically to lead our nation toward fitness than the church. Its very reason for being is to lead people toward spiritual-mental-physical fitness and health.

> Fitness is part of our salvation.
> Fitness in the theological sense is total fitness, body-mind-spirit.
> Fitness is not perfection or diet fads and exercise gimmicks; it is a process of self-management according to God's purposes.
> Fitness is good stewardship of our personhood, our resources, our environment.
> Fitness is a significant part of our proclamation of the gospel.

WHO BETTER THAN CLERGY TO LEAD THE WAY TOWARD FITNESS?

Clergy are the ideal group to guide people toward fitness. Or at least we used to be. But we now exhibit approximately the same statistics of unfitness as the general population, and we need fit lifestyles as much as our parishioners do. Further, how can we preach-teach-counsel salvation (wholeness) when our personal habits subvert this message?

An epidemic of burnout, depression, role confusion, and physical-mental ills plagues our profession. Further, we are targeted for abuse by spiritually unhealthy parishioners in nearly one-half of our congregations (see my earlier book, *Clergy Killers: Guidance for Pastors and Congregations under Fire*, 1997). Obviously many of us are in poor condition to lead believers toward spiritual-mental-physical health. We can do better than this. Thank God, more and more pastors are on a fitness quest!

In the past few years the medical profession has been leading the way toward awareness and the practice of health and fitness. Many people are also calling for a reawakening of faith as a primary ingredient in healing and health. The bestseller lists include books by prominent psychiatrists who discuss spiritual health and faith. Thank God for their ministry, but isn't there something wrong with this picture? While many of us clergy are trying to cope with declining church membership statistics and general triage, or trying to figure which new church growth guru to follow, we are missing the prime ingredient of healthy pastoral ministry: salvation of body and mind and spirit.

SUMMARY

Our case studies were of pastors who recognized their unfitness and responded with a fitness quest, which in two cases brought notable benefits. One pastor, who established body-mind-spirit fitness even while managing disabilities, demonstrates that fitness is for ordinary, limited pastors. And a pastor who turned away from fitness opportunities sank back into dysfunctional unfitness. The unfitness-fitness quizzes should have focused you on your personal data, and the three general questions probed reasons for pursuing body-mind-spirit fitness.

This material prepares us to explore the contexts for our fitness quest: alarming health and fitness statistics, and clergy and congregational vulnerabilities to sickness and dysfunction. Now I will begin to explore prescriptions to cure unfitness by looking at two powerful motivations for a fitness quest in chapters 2 and 3.

2

Clergy Fitness Context

> The healthy society, like the healthy body,
> is not the one that has taken the most medicine.
> It is the one in which the internal health
> building force is in the best shape.
> *Peter Senge*

We live in a culture of unfitness—in society, in the church. And most of us participate willingly in that culture. In fact, we have come to regard our unfitness as normal. Now we don't even know how physically-mentally-spiritually sick we are becoming, because our condition seems so normal.

Our wake-up calls on such unfitness are still too muted to force us to change, but the negative consequences are mounting. A wave of concern and reawakening is beginning to build in our nation, as we realize what health statistics are telling us. Here are a few culled from the Center for Disease Control, American Heart Association, and the U.S. Surgeon General:

> $1 trillion was spent on health care in the United States in 1997 (much of this was unnecessary).

> $40 million was spent on weight-loss programs in 1997 (80 percent regain the weight; 12 percent get fatter; 8 percent change eating habits and stay leaner).

> 55 percent of Americans are overweight; 62 percent do little exercise (since 1978, 72 percent of Americans aged 50 to 69 have become more obese).

> Americans rank twenty-second in the world in longevity and have more heart disease, cancer, stroke, diabetes than in any other country (having the most advanced medical resources in the world does not save us from ourselves).

98 million Americans have high LDL cholesterol levels; 50 million have high blood pressure (much of this could be prevented with lifestyle changes).

$26 billion was spent on heart-bypass surgery and angioplasty in 1997 (80 percent of bypass patients reclog in seven years; 33 percent of angioplasty recipients reclog in six months).

51 million Americans have mental disorders; 17 million are seriously depressed.

Do we need to remind ourselves that clergy have approximately the same health profile as the average American?

Clearly we clergy are in need of healing and a transformation of our lifestyles. But before that will occur, we must realize that the quoted statistics of illness and costs are statistics of sickness . . . of unfitness, not of normalcy. We have become so accustomed to expecting a physician to give us a pill or do a surgical procedure to rescue us from the consequences of our indulgent habits that we seem not to understand that lifestyle changes cost so much less, and feel so much better. "Consciousness-raising" is an outdated term, but it once indicated a dawning awareness of danger and led to positive change. "Attitude," a more current term, indicates a frame of mind governing thinking and behavior. We need both consciousness-raising and an attitude of positive change before healing and transformation can occur. No physician can heal us or keep us healthy. We must do this for ourselves. No mental health professional can cure our denial and illusions. We must do this ourselves. No pastor or guru can make us healthy spiritually. We must do this ourselves.

FROM SICKNESS TO HEALTH

"Woe is me! I am lost, for I am a man of unclean lips, and I live among a people of unclean lips; yet my eyes have seen . . . the Lord of hosts!" These words from Isaiah 6:5 reflect what happens to us when we realize our unfitness and see what we should be. This vision of Isaiah reminds us that we easily forget what fitness is when we lose the vision of health. As with Isaiah, cleansing and transformation is then required to bring us again into obedience to God's purposes for our bodies, minds, and spirits. Following this comes an awareness of our calling, and God's clear direction for our mission.

Healing and recovery are not as automatic as they might seem. Health is a choice, and fitness is a discipline. Our bodies, minds, and spirits have a natural tendency to heal themselves and stay healthy. Yet it does not follow that we can "do what comes naturally" and remain healthy. For we have been conditioned by consumerism and indulgence ("if it feels good, do it") so completely that many of our normal habits are now counterproductive to health. Our body-mind-spirit fitness can accommodate excesses and toxins within certain limits. But when we live indulgent and excessive lifestyles our body-mind-spirit fitness begins to break down. If the violations become chronic, so does the sickness. There are penalties for transgressing the purposes for which God created our bodies, minds, and spirits.

"Do you not know that your body is a temple of the Holy Spirit within you, which you have from God, and that you are not your own? For you were bought with a price; therefore glorify God in your body" (1 Cor. 6:19–20).

Part of our denial process is imagining that we can become fit in one part of ourselves while remaining flabby in the others. This ignores one of the basic principles of biblical wholeness, namely, that body-mind-spirit are interactive and interdependent. There is no such condition as being fit only in spirit or mind or body. All three either support each other's shared fitness or suffer from each other's sickness. One illusion I often encounter in counseling with pastors is that if there are sincere intentions and spiritual fervor, then it won't matter if the body is allowed to become flabby and the mind intoxicated with unhealthy thoughts. Equally wrong are the ideas that a brilliant mind can compensate for an unfit body and spirit, or a gorgeous body for an unfit mind and spirit.

Each of us has idiosyncrasies, limits, and even handicaps, some more than others. And some have disabilities of body or mind or spirit while the other parts are relatively free from abnormalities. The vision of fitness offered here is not one of perfection, but one of realistic fitness that includes our limitations while encouraging the fullest development of what we have. Fitness is not about muscles, marathoning, and physical beauty, it is about being the best that we can be.

Given the present condition of unfitness, most of us will need some kind of healing in order to get started on a fitness quest. We have three options when we are in need of healing. We may interfere with healing and abet sickness and disability. We may simply stop making ourselves sick and get out of the way of natural healing. Or we may facilitate healing. The healing process will be discussed more fully in chapter 4.

In this book I urge a crusade, a churchwide initiative to facilitate healing, and an individual quest for body-mind-spirit fitness among clergy and all spiritual leaders. For it is apparent that many pastors, like their parishioners, have allowed themselves to become unhealthy—unfit in body-mind-spirit. This disables them from leading a congregation into health and fitness. Further, the book of Acts and church history teach us that if spiritual leaders are fully fit, God will lead us in appropriate new directions necessary for our contemporary world.

Our fitness quest begins with an openness to healing and higher states of health, which means a readiness to accept healing and do what is needed to facilitate it. Next comes an adequate understanding of our unfitness, much as salvation begins with an awareness of our sinful condition. This means "naming our demon," to use theological argot. We need to confess our unfitness in a way specific enough for a prescription to be written. For example, "I eat too much junk food," or "I do not study new ideas enough," or "I need to do more spiritual disciplines." Such confessions not only tell us what is wrong, they contain a prescription. This will not be adequate to effect change, of course, but it is the starting place. We must then follow our newfound openness and awareness with the *three dynamics of change:* motivation, decision making, and action. Many of us have learned the necessary steps toward healing and recovery through programs such as Alcoholics Anonymous or by studying scripture and theology. Knowledge and good intentions are never enough, however, nor are guilt trips. But when we begin a commitment toward health and fitness, we are ready then to put our distractions, vulnerabilities, and abuses in useful perspective.

CONFLICTS, DISTRACTIONS, AND VULNERABILITIES

On our fitness quest we need to recognize the terrain we are traversing. As in the religious classic *Pilgrim's Progress,* there are obstacles all along our way.

CONFLICTS

One category of contemporary obstacles for pastors is the conflicting expectations for the pastoral role. You may wish to add to the following lists of expectations.

THE CONGREGATION'S EXPECTATIONS

Though each congregation has its own expectations for a pastor, there is a generic list common to most:

> Be a good preacher—preach the Word, but don't make us uncomfortable.
>
> Be a good teacher—teach us and our children what we want to learn.
>
> Be there when we need you—crises, death, special events.
>
> Don't do things that embarrass us.
>
> Be a CEO, a therapist, a computer specialist, a community leader, a negotiator, a problem-solver, a fund-raiser, and keep our church looking nice and operating well.

THE PASTOR'S EXPECTATIONS

And, of course, pastors have their own expectations.

> All of the above, except for wanting to preach, teach, call, and lead in ways that I think they need, without making them angry at me
>
> An adequate financial package, workable equipment, and a compatible administrative assistant
>
> Parishioners' support of my programs, and if there is conflict, of me in helpful and effective ways
>
> Respect in my denomination
>
> Respect and happiness for my spouse and family here

Such expectations, though normal, are self-centered and can distract us from a clear sense of our calling and fitness quest. I find that the loss of a clear sense of God's call is an early warning sign of unfitness.

Parishioners and pastors have other expectations, of course. But those listed will suffice to make the point of how traditional and inadequate the church's expectations are in a changing world. There are also contemporary distractions that influence our fitness quest substantially.

CONTEMPORARY DISTRACTIONS

Entitlement Thinking. This term does not refer to welfare programs or social justice, but rather to a widespread attitude of our day. Growing evidence indicates that people now feel entitled to whatever they want in life. And if they don't get it, they feel they have a right to blame someone and punish him or her or the organization responsible. There is some value in this attitude: people are willing to act on their own behalf rather than suffer or accept what is perceived as injustice. The downside is the self-centeredness, the excuse for using violence or abuse to get what we want or to punish perceived enemies. This attitude, which pastors share, tends to distract pastors into thinking their lot is unfair. Not a good attitude for a fitness quest.

Consumerism. Closely related to the entitlement attitude is consumerism. Producing, buying, and selling merchandise is part of what has made our nation great, of course. But undisciplined consumerism sets us up for self-indulgence and a denial of the consequences of overeating and overspending—consumerism. In terms of health, we now expect that we can buy a pill to remedy any ill, whether we pay any attention to our health and fitness or not. Instead of asking first, "What does God want?" we more commonly ask, "What do I want?" or "What do my parishioners want?" Consumerism affects pastors and their fitness quests.

Ethics of Consequences. Our world is making a major shift from an ethics rooted in determinative beliefs to an ethics of consequences. Previously people were known by the belief systems that guided their behavior. Though people still pay lip service to some beliefs, most major and minor decisions are now made on the basis of the desired results. Negatively, this distracts us into pseudo dialogues and arguments over who and what is right and wrong. Positively, the consequences of our behavior can guide us into fitness.

Secularization. Public opinion polls indicate that the vast majority of people still believes in God, but only a portion attend church, synagogue, or temple regularly. Fewer learn and live by religious creeds. There is more tolerance of nonreligious beliefs and behaviors. And fewer hold pastors in high regard. This distracts pastors by suggesting that they are expendable . . . and maybe unnecessary. Fitness quest anyone?

Designer Religion. For those who still want some form of religious faith in their lives there is a plethora of gurus, shamans, and designers of religion, outside and within organized religion. Glamorous TV religionists, moralizing motivators, proponents of "feel good" psychology, healers, exponents of exotic cults—all entice followers, and the followers of even the more exotic cults face few evident penalties these days. This may distract clergy into competition for the attention of parishioners who have "itching ears" (2 Tim. 4:3, NRSV), and it may make us vulnerable to fitness charlatans, too.

Business Model. American capitalistic democracy has succeeded far beyond expectations. Not only does the American business model dominate world economies and politics, but it now dominates organized religion. When the congregation (and denomination) are operated as a business, parishioners become customers and stockholders. The church becomes a business instead of a mission. And the pastor is forced to function as a CEO or COO. Further, it implies that the congregation or its powerbrokers may hire and fire the pastor at will. This distracts some pastors into trying to be leaders (in the American COO or CEO model) instead of pastors. Others are distracted into placating powerbrokers or self-destructing in confusion, fear, or burnout. Body-mind-spirit fitness can keep us grounded when we live in such an atmosphere.

Empowered Laity. The past generation of church leaders has leaned toward empowering laity or at least allowing laity more power in the church. This has biblical precedence and sounds fair. But we forgot to train many of our laity and hold them accountable for their leadership. The result is that some lay leaders are biblically illiterate, spiritually undisciplined, unaware of denominational polity, and behaviorally challenged. Such leaders are automatic antagonists to the pastor or vulnerable to a pastor's dominance. Undisciplined and empowered (elected or appointed) laity can distract pastors into making "fight, fidget, or flight" choices, rather than offering tough-minded guidance and support for healthy lay leadership. Thank God there are dedicated, informed, and disciplined lay leaders as well as unfit ones. A fitness quest helps pastors and laity alike in their shared leadership responsibilities.

Pastoral Malfeasance. Some pastors are appearing in the news now, not for their noble ministries but for malfeasance. Surveys of clergy show that about one-fourth of clergy have been or are engaged in sexual malfeasance or feel vulnerable to it. Such scandals are a distraction for all of us. Healthy self-discipline and collegial discipline are replaced by embarrassment, defensiveness, and even confusion. A fitness quest is a primary prescription and prophylactic for sexual malfeasance.

Spiritual Warfare. This seemingly archaic term is being resurrected today, not only by fundamentalists and evangelicals but by concerned progressives as well. In the halcyon days of religion following World War II, we forgot that the context of human life is a struggle between good and evil that dates back to the Garden of Eden.

A contemporary and damaging aspect of spiritual warfare is the conflict and abuse occurring within many congregations. Most troubling for clergy is what I call "the clergy killer phenomenon," presumptive and evil attacks on pastors by powerbrokers in the congregation who have given themselves over to an evil agenda in order to eliminate a pastor, or by sycophants who have been seduced into such an agenda. Nearly one-fourth of America's pastors have been or are being fired. The clergy-killer pattern is now obvious, for the person or congregation that abuses its pastor follows an identifiable pattern and has typically done this before. Such terrorism certainly gets a pastor's attention. But it may distract her or him into becoming a victim or a survivor, instead of putting on "the whole armor of God" (Eph. 6:11) and "fighting the good fight of faith" (2 Tim. 6:12). (Note: This phenomenon is discussed fully in my book *Clergy Killers*.) Conflict, abuse, and spiritual warfare require pastors to be fit, lest they became casualties.

These are some of the distractions that drain a pastor's energy and do collateral damage to the church. It is difficult to be the best that we can be in pastoral ministry with distractions this powerful. And it is becoming impossible for denominations and the church at large to function effectively in this nation when so much time and energy must be devoted to mirroring a conflicted and abusive society and dealing with the consequences.

VULNERABILITIES

Legal Vulnerability. This was a wake-up call for many clergy about ten years ago, when the Nally case was headline news in California courts (in this case, parents sued a pastor for malpractice when their son committed suicide while receiving pastoral counseling). There have been hundreds of lawsuits since. The vast majority of cases in which a pastor is a defendant have to do with sexual malfeasance. An attorney I know who specializes in such cases says he knows of two thousand pending cases. The settlements amount to millions of dollars and prison terms for guilty clergy. The resultant human suffering is enormous.

Sexual misconduct is only one of the legal issues about which we must now be concerned. Church employment and supervision, injury liabilities, violations of civil liberties, taxation issues, and such now may be reviewed by the courts, if there is reason to believe laws have been violated.

I am not an attorney, but from my study and experience with court cases I can suggest that there is reason for concern but not panic about the intrusion of courts, legislatures, and lawyers in pastoral ministry, at least for pastors and organizations not guilty of misdemeanors or felony misconduct. After a brief period in which the courts and lawyers seemed willing to accept any charges against pastors, there is reluctance now. The courts have begun to reject cases in which they may be required to pass judgment on church polity and pastoral practice, citing separation of church and state (First Amendment to the U.S. Constitution), unless there appears to be criminal wrongdoing. Given the litigious attitude in the United States, however, pastors should pay close attention to the denomination's polity and congregational bylaws and stay informed regarding relevant legislation and court decisions. Ministering according to denominational polity, congregational bylaws, and sound theology is a good defense.

It is a good idea to consult with an attorney who specializes in issues relevant to clergy and the church when you have questions. And it will be helpful for pastors to read "Church Law and Tax Report" (published by Christian Ministry Resources, Matthews, N.C.). This bimonthly newsletter reports on all court cases involving clergy and religious organizations. Being informed about legal issues and achieving body-mind-spirit fitness are ways to manage legal vulnerability competently.

Ethical Vulnerability. The "ethics of consequences" paradigm shift in our world has already been mentioned as a distraction. It is also an area of vulnerability for pastors. General loss of sincerely held beliefs and practices, along with loss of respect for clergy, make it dangerous for a pastor to take a moral stand that is not endorsed by the congregation, or at least by its powerbrokers. But we have recently received significant guidance through the panicky but typically competent process by which denominations and religious organizations have devised, and usually enforce, codes of conduct for clergy. Unfortunately, little has been done to apply and enforce such codes for laity. But hopeful signs are emerging. For example, the Presbyterian Church (U.S.A.), at its 210th General Assembly (1998), approved a new "Standards of Ethical Conduct" code applicable to clergy, elders, and to lay members and volunteer workers in PC(USA) congregations uniformly.

Pastors are vulnerable to accusations of "boundary violations," whether true or false. Sometimes we are the victims and sometimes the perpetrators in moral and ethical misconduct. Sometimes we are caught in ethical binds, as in confidentiality issues, or in the disharmony between traditional beliefs and contemporary realities. And sometimes ethical issues reveal more of our biases and prejudices than we are willing to admit. Fitness helps.

Professional Vulnerability. Besides the legal and ethical vulnerabilities mentioned, there is a more general professional vulnerability for pastors. We are discovering that the shrinkage in most major denominations is leaving us with fewer viable pastorates. Thus we are vulnerable to competitiveness and being without call. We are vulnerable to the confusion that comes with massive social change, which always affects the role of the clergy, whether we are leading it or trying to be neutral and uncontroversial. And finally, we are vulnerable to our professional training. As clergy, we were trained in the academic model, which has become less relevant in an experientially oriented society. In the resultant feelings of inadequacy we tend to seek remedial training in management skills, conflict resolution, social diversity control, computerized ministry, counseling competence, and such. These are all valuable. Yet we are having difficulty as a profession in determining what our contemporary role really is. This makes us vulnerable in a variety of spiritual, mental, and physical ways. Fitness helps.

As the realities of our unfitness and vulnerabilities sweep over us, we are in danger of despair or random flounderings. So it is important that we turn our attention now to a more positive view of where we are headed on our fitness quest.

FITNESS IS AN ADVENTURE

We could say that body-mind-spirit fitness is our obligation, our goal, our responsibility, our mandate. But such thinking tends to trigger resistance, guilt trips, or New Year's resolutions, none of which produce the desired result. Instead, we can think of our personal fitness as an adventure. This kind of thinking can bypass our excuses by tapping into the natural tendency of healthy human minds toward curiosity, creativity, and growth, along with our desire to feel, look, work, and play better. However, this adventure is not about playful, euphoric escapades, but about the serious, worthwhile transformation of unhealthy lifestyles and ministries, accompanied by a powerful partner for transformation, namely, attitude—positive attitude. "Positive thinking" (Norman Vincent Peale), and "possibility thinking" (Robert Schuller) are attitudes that can be helpful. Both of these have value, but they tend to offer a bootstrap optimism that may not be adequate for the serious transformation needed for moving from unfitness to fitness.

Adventure thinking, instead, is an attitude of openness to God's transforming grace through the intentional acceptance of physical, mental, and spiritual disciplines in order to facilitate fitness. In addition we add an attitude of thankfulness, which is a celebrative and appreciative spirit that savors the escalating joy that accrues when we are the best that we can be, in our various stages of development.

Most of us need some kind of map or mental image of the adventure we desire, lest we flounder. You can probably think of a desirable and pleasurable achievement or intentional growth project in your past that can give you clues about this present adventure. If not, perhaps you can remember an adventure by someone else that attracted you. If neither of these are available, you can craft a totally new adventure by mixing appropriate ingredients and seeking advice and support from mentors and valued friends.

The guidelines for making the fitness quest into an adventure are the dynamic ingredients that can keep the commitment and disciplines of the fitness lifestyle from becoming drudgery. Achieving fitness requires some hard work to begin with, and then a disciplined lifestyle that becomes increasingly comfortable and valuable. The adventure attitude makes our commitment and effort more stimulating because of the way we think and work toward fitness.

Perhaps the "vision quest" practiced by some Native American tribes is a useful metaphor. In its primary form the vision quest occurred when a young man was taken to a location isolated from his tribe. He was expected to live off the land and survive alone for a period, as a way of learning the meaning of his life. The tribe expected that the lessons of this time of self-reliance would guide a young man into responsible citizenship and leadership. The fitness quest I suggest here has similar dynamics and consequences. For we learn from our own experience how to put the knowledge about fitness that we are learning into practice. This is essentially an individual experience. But we are not alone in the larger sense, for our Creator is with us, and our intimates (family, spouse, close friends) and the community of faith appreciate and support the fitness quest. And hopefully, all have or will someday have their own fitness quest for personal and community benefit.

A worthy adventure has four ingredients: curiosity, exploration, discovery, and transformation.

Curiosity: "I wonder what will happen if I . . . "
"I am anxious to see if I can do this."
"I want to learn how to do this."

There is a healthy and exciting use of imagination in adventuring, for we will do part of our exploring mentally. This allows us to try possibilities in our minds before and after the physical acts of exploring fitness. Our imagination also allows us to bypass some intimidating habit barriers and to either encourage or discourage ourselves by what we imagine.

Exploration: investigating, researching, experimenting, assessing, doing

The foundation blocks for healthy exploration are confidence in oneself, belief in God's purposes, and trust in derived information and support resources. The exploration process is the actual work of the fitness, and it is exhilarating, tiring, satisfying, boring, reassuring, and confusing all at the same time. All the steps in our exploration of personal and corporate fitness lead us into valuable new territory.

Discovery: finding newness, achievement, weakness, strengths, insight, potential

The work of the fitness adventure is satisfying at the deepest levels of human experience. For we develop insight (understanding), strengths, meanings, values, and relationships in significant new ways. Even if we fail to achieve the highest levels of fitness, we will learn much of value and lay groundwork for further exploration and adventure.

Transformation: opening or growing ourselves to be the best that we can be

There is mystery and magic about transformation, for it means moving beyond present forms and limits—metamorphosis. Transformation can move toward negative or positive change. Though our bodies, minds, and spirits tend toward health, healing, and growth, the potential for sickness, unfitness, deterioration, and death is also present. Positive transformation requires careful thought and spiritual disciplines. Our minds are the most conscious and manageable personal resource we have as we participate in transformation. The apostles Paul and Peter give urgent appeals for us to use our minds to participate in needed transformation of our personhood (Rom. 12:1–2) and to grow in grace (Eph. 4:15, 2 Peter 3:18). Along with the example of fitness in Jesus Christ, the appeals of the greatest apostles give us a biblical incentive to be the best that we can be—to undertake a fitness adventure, a fitness quest

QUESTIONS ABOUT FITNESS

Now let us return to two of the motivational questions I asked in chapter 1 and answer them from a slightly different perspective. These are the two most important questions in this book. You will need to answer them convincingly or you are unlikely to proceed despite your best efforts.

WHY SHOULD I BE INTERESTED IN FITNESS?

1. The benefits are enormous.
2. It's not that hard, really.
3. It is less and less likely that we can survive the rigors of contemporary pastoring if we are unfit.
4. Fitness is not perfectionism.
5. Fitness is our best stewardship.

Think about this question and these answers with me.

1. The benefits are enormous. This is not hyperbole, for fitness is not simply a good idea—it feels great, looks good, and works beautifully. As you make the transition from unfitness to fitness, you will notice immediate benefits. You will be pleased with yourself for doing something positive about your less-than-fit condition, instead of merely wishing and hoping and envying those who are fit. Soon you will have more energy and you will feel stronger, more confident, more efficient. You will waste less time playing mental games with yourself or feeling angry and frustrated and confused. Your new fitness lifestyle will cost you less. For as you establish a healthy nutritional, work, recreation, and relational regimen, you will spend less on junk food, alcohol, coping mechanisms, and unnecessary clutter and stuff. People will notice your fitness and begin to think of you differently. And it is likely that you will become a fitness model for the physical-mental-spiritual yearnings and needs of parishioners and colleagues. Why not be the first to achieve fitness in your home territory instead of the last?

2. It's not that hard, really. This answer is important because part of being unfit is having excuses for not becoming fit. When I occasionally have self-doubts or wonder if my daily fitness regimens are worth the

effort, I remind myself that I don't have to be perfect, nor do I have to struggle and strain in order to be fit. I simply follow my simple, daily fitness pattern and let the satisfactions and successes of being fit reassure me. I am learning to try smarter instead of harder.

When you read the chapters on the specific exercises, disciplines, and celebrations of fitness, you will see that physical fitness requires only simple changes in nutrition, exercise, work, and rest habits. Mental fitness requires only some simple changes in attitude, reframing of thought patterns, relaxed decision making, and mental growth exercises. Spiritual fitness requires only an analysis of how effective your present spiritual disciplines are in nurturing you spiritually, and then considering some fresh ways to enjoy union-communion with God, nature, and other persons.

We do not need to become fitness nerds in order to be physically-mentally-spiritually fit. Many of us have forgotten (or never learned) how simple and natural fitness is. It is a matter of living the way God intended us to live and enjoying every minute of it.

3. It is less and less likely that we can survive the rigors of contemporary pastoring if we are unfit. It is the endemic debilitation among clergy today that is making us vulnerable to the pressures, abuses, and misconceptions that are robbing us of the joy of ministry. Moreover, when we are unfit we are more likely to be overwhelmed by the criticisms, abuses, tough decisions, and inertia of spiritually sick congregations, all of which are now normal in pastoring. We will tend to second-guess ourselves, whip ourselves, strain to please everyone, and neglect the very things that make for health.

4. Fitness is not perfectionism. We are human beings, with human limitations and potentials. We can grow and enjoy the human pilgrimage without sabotaging it with perfectionism. Being the best that you can be is a matter of being yourself, with a clear understanding of how you can become better.

5. Fitness is our best stewardship. The most important reason to continue our fitness quest is that this is what God created us to do. Like the servants who were given various numbers of talents (Matt. 25:14–30), we each have physical-mental-spiritual personhood and resources for which each is responsible to God. The joy of living and ministry is greatest when we live out the fitness for which we were created.

WHY SHOULD THE CHURCH BE CONCERNED
ABOUT FITNESS?

1. Organized religion is not responding adequately to the needs of an unfit society.

2. Clergy are losing respect, are being abused, are stressed, and know that many of us are not in condition to be moral-spiritual leaders in a confused, spiritually debilitated world.

3. To be successful, efforts to "reinvent" the church must be built upon a basic spiritual-mental-physical fitness or they will not have the power to lead us toward God's purposes.

Think about this question and these answers with me.

1. Organized religion is not responding adequately to the needs of an unfit society. The vast majority of Americans believe in God and that God is active in our lives. Yet there is a steady decline in active congregational participation. Public opinion polls, along with lists of best-selling books, indicate that moral-spiritual issues are a primary concern of Americans. This suggests a deep spiritual yearning and searching that is not satisfied by traditional religion. Presently these needs simply go unmet or generate an urgent search for nurture among the gurus, pop psychologists, and designers of religion.

2. Clergy are losing respect. Not only has the general public lost much of the confidence formerly expressed regarding clergy, we clergy are losing confidence in ourselves and our role in society. I have found that a majority of pastors feel inadequate to the task of moral-spiritual leadership. A growing number of us are depressed, burned out, and exhibiting the signs of unhealthiness, which are: asking lots of "why" questions, being cynical about the church, anxiously seeking for quick fixes, being overweight and out of shape, having unhappy spouses.

There is no one to rescue us—except ourselves, with support and guidance from God and colleagues, if we ask. Yet this is good news. For we now realize we are in charge of our condition and our ministry. My favorite word for describing how we can take responsibility for ourselves is *disintermediation*. This is a term borrowed from economics and sociology. It means taking our investments from a place of low returns and putting them where there is more direct control and profit, or getting rid of unnecessary intermediaries in our lives. I like this term because it is unusual and gets our attention. It is common for us to become so dependent upon unnecessary resources and relationships that we fail to notice how these have become distractions or codependencies rather than being helpful. Part of our fitness quest is cleaning up our lives and clearing out debris and "stuff." Then we can get serious about fitness.

3. To be successful, efforts to "reinvent" the church must be built upon a basic spiritual-mental-physical fitness or they will not have the

power to lead us toward God's purpose. Band-Aids won't heal body-mind-spirit unhealthiness. A basic condition of fitness is necessary. Thank God, healing, nurture, and wholeness are readily available. But these are not automatic. Such fitness requires the kind of body-mind-spirit transformations that have long been part of our salvation. Yet they must now be achieved in ways appropriate to our contemporary needs and situations. This is our fitness quest. Thanks be to God.

SUMMARY

The dire state of health and fitness in the United States focuses our attention on the seriousness of our shared condition, and the serious dysfunctions of congregations and pastors force clergy to put the sickness context at our doorstep. Our generic questions about why we should be vitally interested in body-mind-spirit fitness now have a context that underscores their importance. We began to bridge the gap between awareness and change by offering the two attitudes that provide positive motivation for change: a spirit of adventure and the freeing process of disintermediation. All of this work prepares us for a careful analysis of the ingredients in body-mind-spirit fitness in chapter 3.

3

The ABCs of Fitness

> Wholeness or well being is not the
> absence of brokenness. Instead it is what
> you choose, at the center of your life,
> to do with your brokenness.
> *Howard Clinebell*

Some clarifications are appropriate now, for though the language used so far has been familiar, when applied to fitness it is used in distinctive ways. Further, though each health-related term used here has its own meaning, these terms are inextricably intertwined. "Fitness" and its cognate terms (health, wellness, soundness, wholeness, and such) are prodigious and complicated concepts. And since they are common terms, they come loaded with misconceptions as well as helpful implications. Therefore they need definition and analysis if we are to apply them to ordinary human experience. The following definitions are not exhaustive but are simply how I use these terms in this book.

IMPORTANT DEFINITIONS

Health. This is the generic term for a normally functioning human body. But it is also used to describe normalcy of mind and spirit. This term is so generic that it is used, with adjectives, to describe the present condition of a person—"poor health," "excellent health," "deteriorating health." It is most typically used, however, to indicate normalcy or soundness. We should remind ourselves that equilibrium, feeling comfortable, and coping are not the same as health and fitness. These can be valuable in themselves. But they often masquerade as signs of health and fitness. Give this some thought.

Wellness. "Wellness" is a contemporary term designed to be used more specifically about health. It is commonly used to indicate a condition of full functioning and soundness and often implies intentionality and discipline, as in "the practice of wellness."

Soundness. This word tends to refer more specifically to body parts that are functioning adequately or even at their highest potential, as in "a sound heart."

Wholeness. Popular jargon claims the word "wholeness," and it often appears as an adjective in, for example, "holistic medicine," "holistic therapy," even "holistic theology." "Holistic" means relating to the whole person, or covering the full range of the subject. When I use the word "wholeness" here I refer to the biblical-spiritual concept of "shalom" and completeness. However, I also use it as a spiritualized term to mean more than a condition. It also means congruency, synergy, blending, and even union-communion with God and all of creation. Shalom, in Hebrew, not only includes completeness, but may be interpreted as "peace" or "salvation" as well.

Wholeness is a dynamic and inspirational word containing deep meanings and broad connotations. As used here, it refers to the totality of a human being: body-mind-spirit. And it includes a conscious and unconscious blending with God's purposes. Wholeness will be described more fully in chapter 4, on healing.

Fitness. Fitness is the central concept in this book. The simplest and briefest definition of fitness is intentional, interactive wellness; the intentional practice of high-level health. By "intentional" I mean a conscious, disciplined pursuit of health and soundness in all parts of a human being. "Intentional" by this definition indicates the conscious, disciplined choice of wellness developed to high functional levels. By "interactive" I refer to interdependency and the dynamic aspects of all the parts as they function together in the organic, rational, and spiritual process of being both a discrete, personal system yet also part of the larger system we call creation. Wellness, I noted above, means functioning fully and fulfilling potential. It does not imply strain and maximal effort, nor heroic accomplishments. Nor does it imply perfection. It simply means functioning at the best possible levels. When I use the terms "fit" and "fitness," I do not mean such things as suitable, approved, proper, confirmed, prepared, and able, although all of these characteristics and qualities may be included in the definition offered here.

"Recombinant fitness" is my full name for this kind of wholistic fitness. The recombinant terminology refers to dynamic interaction of body, mind, and spirit in fitness. This term incorporates factors such as origin, function, and purpose and thus indicates that the fitness discussed in this book is much more, much deeper, than the popular notion of fitness as strong muscles and aerobic capacity. "Recombinant" is a term from biochemistry. It is related to the familiar term "recombinant DNA," which is a central process of genetic engineering in which genetic material that is divided in meiosis is reunited in designed fashion rather than randomly, as in the fertilization of an ovum (egg) or in cell multiplication.

I combine the terms "recombinant" and "fitness" here to remind us that the body-mind-spirit fitness of the fitness quest has its origin in creation and in God's purposes. It reminds us also that these three aspects of humanity—body, mind, and spirit—are homologous in some mysterious and real sense, due to their origin and structure. Yet the function of each is different. When combined they identify a unique individual with characteristics resulting from the interactivity of body, mind, and spirit.

For simplicity and familiarity I use the term "fitness" without further reference to the recombinant terminology. Yet this concept is so important to the kind of fitness I suggest that I hope the body-mind-spirit terminology will remind us of it.

Discipline. Discipline is integral to fitness. Since the term "discipline" carries overtones from tradition and contemporary usage, it needs a definition here, for I use it often. And if it is not understood in this context, it could have a negative influence on a positive concept. In its simplest meaning here, discipline is positive self-management, which includes rationality and emotionality; is oriented toward worthy goals; and means joyful, grace-filled, and satisfying. Self-management here means autogenic behavior guided by conscious strategy. It includes rationality, intuition, and affect.

Discipline also has a secondary meaning here. It refers to a developed regimen, or an already existent pattern of behavior and thinking. This is especially applicable to the use of the term "spiritual disciplines." And again, it will be a positive, joyful concept.

The negative, stoic, and masochistic connotations often implied by the word "discipline" are not part of its definition when used in relationship to fitness in this book. Emphasize positive, joyful, and rewarding meanings of the word "discipline" as you read this book, lest the common, negative connotations trigger a conscious or unconscious resistance to your own fitness quest. This positive meaning is not, however, an invitation to temporary euphoria, casualness, or New Year's resolutions. The practice of disciplined fitness is serious but not cheerless. In fact, it produces one of the deepest and most satisfying senses of well-being and confidence possible for human beings. In its finest expression it is being the best that you can be . . . intentionally.

LEVELS OF FITNESS

Not only do individuals and organizations have different inherent potential for fitness, but all of us function on different levels. I believe there are three levels of fitness.

Level One is the minimum fitness of a person functioning healthfully, and doing what is necessary to sustain this level.

Level Two is highly developed fitness in which a person concentrates on being the best that she or he can be . . . and growing.

Level Three is an intensive fitness effort focused on achieving an extraordinary goal, such as a politician taking on an arduous political campaign, an athlete training for the Olympics, a student studying for final exams, a pastor moving to a difficult congregation. Though level-three fitness is usually concentrated on a sizable mental or spiritual task, the body-mind-spirit combination must have all its components raised to the highest levels of nurture and performance to sustain such an effort. And if the demand for extraordinary performance continues for a long time and exceeds the limits of one's body-mind-spirit poten-tial, collapse, unfitness, and burnout are inevitable.

I encourage you to do your own thinking about the practice of full fitness and to develop your own definitions. But the caveat here is: avoid sabotaging the positive motivations necessary for fitness through conscious or unconscious negativity and bias.

THE ABCS OUTLINE

The ABCs format is a helpful structure that organizes and summarizes information in order to focus on the essentials needed for a particular topic. ABCs also suggest simplicity. I use this outline throughout the book to organize insights and practices of body-mind-spirit fitness.

A–Awareness: What do I know and need to know about fitness? Learn it.

B–Basics: What are basic resources and experiences for my fit-ness? Do them.

C–Congruence: What are basic relationships of fitness? Build and enjoy them.

Now we can expand and discuss this ABCs outline as it applies to body-mind-spirit fitness.

"A" STANDS FOR AWARENESS

By awareness I mean conscious, focused attention. There will be an unconscious, intuitive dimension to such attention, of course. But the emphasis is on the conscious, cognitive dynamic of this term.

To make this important term more experiential, how about trying something? Close your eyes, and keep them closed for a few minutes. Pay attention to what goes on in your mind—your consciousness—as your eyes are closed. Note how your awareness with your eyes closed differs from awareness when they are open. Let this be a metaphor for your awareness. For we will need to apply our visual skills as well as memory, imagination, and intuition when developing our fullest possible awareness of fitness. Without full and intentional awareness, we will be limited to habitual ways of thinking. And if we limit our awareness of fitness to habitual, biased thoughts, there will be no fitness quest.

Jesus often told his listeners to "open your eyes and *see!*" This is a potent reminder of the distortions possible as our mind translates everything our eyes see, and indeed does this for all our sensory data. Recent brain research indicates that though our eyes transmit accurate data from the light waves that impact the retina, our brains transmit this data immediately to interpretation centers, which then tell our conscious minds how to think about this data. Lawyers know this: when they put two witnesses to the same accident on the witness stand in court, they often get two different versions of the event. "Beauty is in the eye of the beholder" is one familiar way to put this idea. And remember comedian Flip Wilson's trademark declaration: "What you see is what you get!" which means don't expect more than is there, but also that we tend to get what we imagine we see, whether real or fantasy.

Understanding and transforming our assumptions and misconceptions about fitness are crucial for a fitness quest. The mental transformation we must make regarding fitness includes five tasks:

1. Identify and discard misconceptions and negative presumptions.
2. Open yourself to new data and experience.
3. Experiment and practice with your fitness program until you get it right for your personal needs and situations and ministries.

4. Celebrate and savor (that is, feel sensual joy) what you then come to experience in your fitness quest.
5. Model and witness to the gospel of fitness of body-mind-spirit.

It is both saddening and maddening to note what has happened to the American psyche regarding fitness, health, and beauty. Our minds are almost uniformly programmed to "see" fitness as big muscles, marathoning capabilities, or gorgeous bodies. The increase in cases of anorexia and bulimia is the worst possible result of such tragic misconceptions. The cosmetic industry, health and nutrition stores, and exercise gimmicks, as well as a biased media, also can rob us of a healthy sense of reality, beauty, and fitness unless we open ourselves to the necessary transformation.

After purging your mind of such stereotypes, you can then insert accurate data, reliable experience, and templates for your fitness regimen and the fitness lifestyle appropriate to ministries that will induce spiritual health instead of the latest designer religion. This redeemed and transformed awareness can guide your fitness quest.

"B" STANDS FOR BASICS

The meaning of "basics" is obvious, except for those subconscious and mysterious ingredients that we can name, but scarcely understand fully. The most obvious basics of fitness are a person, a regimen, performance, consequences. But underlying those are additional basics: personhood, resources, environment, motivations, costs, potential, simplicity, and finally the vision of fitness we have. All of these ingredients are dynamic and interactive.

Personhood, at its heart, indicates the material and immaterial uniqueness of a human being. Body-mind-spirit is the segmented name given to personhood in this book. These are generic terms, of course. So for an identity that completes the personhood we add a name—*your* name, a genome (your genetic base and potential), an *imago Dei* (the image of our Creator—like a trademark), and a vocation (God's purposes for you). Fitness is not about a general condition or some nice idea in the national consciousness, it is *your* fitness. Unique to you; blessed with your gifts and graces; stamped "approved" by God; and with a personal and shared mission. Your individualism, however, has little meaning without other individuals—your intimates and the whole geofamily. Martin Buber taught us that personal identity is incomplete without relationships and the process of shaping those relationships.

Resources of fitness are both obvious and subtle. For example, a bicycle is a resource for fitness, yet it can also be a status symbol (brand name, cost, condition). Energy is a resource, yet even though we all think we know what energy is, no one can define it precisely or even say where it comes from or where it goes. We know that fitness does not occur passively. It requires a dedicated use of energy. Energy comes in four types: physical, mental, emotional, spiritual. Yet even such categories are transient.

Nutrition is a resource. Yet nutrition comes in a variety of forms from the basic food pyramid categories (vegetables, fruits, grains, meats, dairy, fats/oils/sweets), to liquids, to our own concoctions and junk food. And, of course, oxygen and sunlight are also part of nutrition. In places in our nation and the world, severe limits on the availability of food determine much of the nutritional pattern. In such circumstances low physical weight and the conditioning of hard work establish a certain kind of fitness. Fitness is hardly an issue in areas where nutrition is limited to basics, hard work keeps the body and mind in shape, and a cultural religion conditions the spirit. But for most of us abundance and excesses are readily available, and combined with sedentary work and lifestyles, make unfitness likely. Fitness for privileged Americans is a matter of intentional disciplines.

Nurture is the mental-spiritual version of nutrition. It is the caring, supportive nourishing of mind and spirit. Feeding our minds and souls generally receives little conscious attention. We usually do a few things that provide some nurture, but we seldom give this any careful attention. The result is much the same as when we pay little attention to nutrition for our bodies: eating becomes the issue, instead of nutrition. We eat on the run, or eat mostly what tastes good, or eat for entertainment, compensation, or socializing rather than with a realistic plan for meeting our physical needs. When our physical selves receive most of our attention, our minds and spirits become shriveled, distorted, and addicted to whatever satisfies temporarily. Mental and spiritual junk food are as common for Americans as physical junk food, with similar consequences. Happiness and a sense of well-being are more healthfully achieved when mind and spirit are fit, as well as our bodies.

The list of fitness resources is enormous: equipment, materials, exercise, training facilities, money, schools and libraries, consultants, the Internet, Holy Scripture, clergy, sacred places, and meditation. One fitness task is to review and prioritize fitness resources in personal and responsible ways in order to keep it all simple and realistic.

Environment for fitness comprises both limits and potential. Tradition, socialization, facilities, support systems, and such determine our concepts of fitness in obvious and subtle ways. Again, we have individual and shared responsibility for our own fitness and the fitness of others.

I have found it informative to review the biblical stories of the environments in which Bible characters lived out their fitness and unfitness. The Garden of Eden is a fascinating environment in which mental-spiritual unfitness produced monumental consequences. The wanderings from Mesopotamia to Canaan for Abraham, Egypt and the Wilderness for Moses, battlefield and palace for David, exile for prophets, Israel for Jesus, the known world for Paul—reading between the lines indicates that these people lived with various states of fitness and unfitness, as we do. Life in contemporary America and the typical pastoral ministry are quite different from those ancient times, yet the basics of body-mind-spirit fitness are much the same.

Motivations for fitness are the engines that drive it: creativity, attitude, energy, stimulation, emotions, an activated regimen, reinforcement, and the anticipation of future consequences. Note that potent term "disintermediation" as it relates to motivation. Intermediation means shifting the responsibilities for our personal behavior and condition onto others. Disintermediation, here, means that we recognize that no one else can make us healthy and fit. This is our personal responsibility and our joy. Motivation will be discussed more fully later.

Costs of fitness are both obvious and obscure. The dollars spent, the time dedicated to fitness regimens, and the energy used are obvious costs and should be calculated at the beginning of a fitness quest, and periodically when fitness becomes a way of life. The more obscure costs are the time taken from other possible tasks, the consequences for other persons, and the costs to the environment. When figuring the costs of fitness, however, it is critically important to calculate or at least estimate the costs of unfitness for comparison, because physical and mental health statistics and what we can know of effects of our spiritual health indicate that body-mind-spirit unfitness is considerably more costly than fitness.

We need to be realistic about the costs of both fitness and unfitness, for the potential for self-deception exists. The beginning stages of our fitness quest are fraught with mind games. In a typical game we argue back and forth within ourselves about whether or not we feel like doing our exercise routine today, or we should eat a handful of grapes instead of a candybar halfway through the afternoon, or we should establish a regular time at the library instead of watching so much TV, or we should reevaluate our meditative practices versus letting them become boring. In our business-dominated society there is a tendency to think of costs mostly in terms of dollars, time, and energy. Fitness, however, is best thought of in terms of health, effectiveness, and stewardship.

Potential has to do with opportunities, possibilities, and limits. Opportunities are made as often as bestowed, as we know. Translated into the fitness motif, this means that waiting for fitness to happen or for the perfect time to begin a fitness quest is fruitless. "Just do it" isn't a bad slogan. Or try "Choose fitness." Opportunities for fitness abound. Missing them is costly.

Shakespeare said it well:

There is a tide in the affairs of men,
Which, taken at the flood, leads on to fortune;
Omitted, all the voyage of their life
Is bound in shallows and in miseries.
                    (*Julius Caesar*, 4.3.218)

The possibilities for personal fitness are greater than we usually think. So are the benefits. Robert Schuller's "possibility thinking" may be useful here. For unless we "push the envelop" and "think outside the box," we may either overestimate or underestimate our possibilities.

When fitness is real rather than a fantasy, it has both possibilities and limits. The farther we grow into the satisfactions of fitness, the more we must cope with the frustrations of limits —physical, mental, spiritual, as well as relational and financial. But limits are a hallmark of our humanity and limits can change; illness, accidents, changed situations, and aging all alter our limits. A healthy characteristic of fitness is learning to deal with present and coming limits appropriately.

Simplicity is a subjective ingredient I have added to the basics because it is necessary as a corrective to our prevalent "more is better" way of thinking. Fitness is not an add-on, not a Band-Aid, not a quick fix for all that is wrong. Fitness is simple, realistic stewardship of our personhood. This principle of simplicity was modeled (Matt. 8:20) and taught by Jesus (Matt. 5:37; Mark 10:28–30; Luke 12:22–34) and reaffirmed by the apostle Paul (Phil. 4:11). In nineteenth-century philosophy, Occam's razor, or the law of parsimony, urged that when there are options, we should choose the simplest one. We are now learning that accumulating things, habits, relationships, and obligations complicates and stresses our lives beyond our capacity to manage them well. Cutting back and living within limits is part of fitness. It takes a fit mind, spirit, and body to cut through life's complications in order to find simplicity. It means we must give up some seemingly attractive rewards, but we gain peace of mind and the real possibility that we can concentrate on body-mind-spirit fitness.

Vision is a magical word that applies readily to fitness and our fitness quest. Having a vision is a result of thinking. How we *think* about fitness and our fitness quest is vitally important. A mental picture of what we will do for fitness and how we will look and feel can motivate or discourage us. Further, the mission for our fitness gives it meaning.

Though I discussed thinking under "Awareness" and will explain it later in the section on mental fitness, emphasizing how we think about fitness is also appropriate here. We all know that we think with our minds, but we may not realize that our bodies and spirits affect thinking too. They interact with and influence our mind. The cognitive process itself needs examination periodically, if we expect to be fit mentally. For our minds think all the time, whether we tell them to or not.

Recent research is demonstrating something new to many, namely, that our hearts are more than pumps. They also think. So do our other organs, and even our cells. But such thinking is different from and yet part of the total thought process of human beings. As the Bible and poets have long known, the heart is the seat of our emotions and may be the basic site for our souls. This is the affective (emotion) part of cognition, which teams with the rational process our brains do. Most of us experience this blend as conscious thoughts, along with feelings and intuitions. Sometimes we think one way but feel something else. This demonstrates the two aspects of cognition. We have both mind and heart to provide both, but we tend to believe or trust one more than the other. When we allow one to dominate and exclude the other, we limit our awareness.

Research on the human heart as a thinking organ is relatively new and quite different from the research on the human brain, which we understand a little better; there is not enough space here to explore this fascinating subject. For more information about the heart and its mode of thinking, explore Paul Pearsall's book, *The Heart's Code*, and Doc Childre and Howard Martin's book, *The HeartMath Solution*, which are listed in the bibliography. Pearsall presents the massive research being done on the thinking heart, while Childre and Martin offer guidance for incorporating more of the heart's emotional thinking into our behavior.

Most of us are not trained to be aware of our thought processes. Part of fitness will be "taking time to think about how we are thinking, about what we are thinking about." This conundrum is a useful way of alerting ourselves to the value of catching ourselves in the act of thinking.

If you are not practiced in the skill of watching yourself think, you may need to devise a way to do so. One is to keep a daily journal of your conscious thoughts, along with attempts to note when you thought them, and what unconscious thoughts they imply. You may decide to use an awareness device such as that described in Herbert Benson's *Relaxation Response* (see the bibliography). Basically, you assume a relaxed position and with eyes closed focus on deep breathing until your mind is cleared enough to become aware of single thoughts and the management of each thought. Another exercise called "freeze-frame" is similar but focuses on the heart (see bibliography: Doc Childre and Howard Martin, *HeartMath Solution*). Biofeedback training is another way to become aware of thinking. The use of an algorithm (chart) listing sequential thoughts that lead to a distinct conclusion is also useful. And you can simply ask yourself to notice the consequences of your behavior or to answer the question, "Why am I thinking and acting like this?" The power of thinking over our behavior is the reason we use slogans to guide our behavior. This book and the fitness movement are full of slogans, such as "Fitness is good stewardship" (FIGS); "Eat smart;" "Fitness is an attitude;" "Health is a choice, fitness is a discipline;" "Unfitness is your privilege, but everybody's bill."

There are three levels, or capacities, of thinking.

Think-1 is the primary, automatic level of thinking, the thinking we do without thinking. This includes the thinking done by mind, heart, and body.

Think-2 is creative thinking, which usually comes in unpredictable, induced, or spontaneous bursts. This also includes the resources of mind, heart, and body.

Think-3 is a learned skill of thinking creatively, at will and often. This level includes learning, intuition, and spiritual discernment. We can learn to function at this highest level of thinking more consistently as part of fitness. It will be most complete when it includes the perceptions and conclusions coming from our minds, hearts, and bodies, and is tuned to God's purposes through God's gift of discernment.

As I mentioned, the conscious image we have of fitness—particularly of our own personal fitness—is important to the fitness quest. Using mental imagery, conscious or unconscious, can lead us to reproduce that same image in real-life experiences. For example, several Olympic coaches some years ago revolutionized athletic training by teaching their pupils to envision doing their athlete feat perfectly, and imagining that so precisely that their bodies then began to follow this mental picture as a recipe for improvement. Such training dramatically improved athletic performance over a performance shaped only by repetition and practice. This envisioning process has been translated into other fields, and, of course, is not unknown to visionaries in the Bible.

Yet another aspect of visioning is recognizing the mission or goal of the vision. This has to do with motivation and with meaning. We are much more likely to proceed satisfactorily into fitness when we feel the outcome and application of our fitness are desirable and worthwhile. Fitness used for God's purposes qualifies as such motivation. So does feeling good, enjoying a healthy body, watching ourselves do well, and accepting compliments from those who appreciate our fitness.

Healing is basic to fitness. Healing clears the decks for fitness. The healing required for fitness is more than a simple recovery of health. It is the awareness of need and potential, the use of this basic transformation of body-mind-spirit in the fitness quest, and the recovery, repair, and installation of relationships necessary for body-mind-spirit fitness. This broader understanding of healing will be discussed fully in chapter 4, on healing.

Attitude undergirds but also limits nearly all aspects of fitness. Attitude is the conscious and subconscious living out of beliefs, interpretations, and habits developed over the course of life. Like the programming in a computer, it limits and defines our actions. Though there is potential for much more, our attitude sets the pathways and boundaries of the program. The writer of the program can revise it, within the structural possibilities of the computer. When the programmer learns what is useful and what is counterproductive in the program, it can be changed. This is similar to what we do in developing and revising the basic attitudes by which we make our decisions and live our lives. It should be apparent then that your attitude toward life, your environment, your potential, and your fitness must be revised in order for all resources and structures to be guided toward body-mind-spirit fitness. Attitude is a negative factor in the fitness quest when it is shaped by fear and resistance. It is a positive factor when it is shaped by openness, an understanding of fitness as good stewardship, and by the excitement in seeing and feeling the benefits of fitness. It is important, then, to recognize your personal attitude toward fitness and revise it in ways that allow you to grow into full fitness.

"C" STANDS FOR CONGRUENCY

This term means relationship, interdependence, interaction, blending, harmony, unity. Congruency is important in the ABCs schema because it mandates serious consideration of what the Awareness and Basics factors mean in relationship to everything else. Nothing exists by itself, not even God. For fitness this means not only that our body, mind, and spirit are a unity, but that fitness must include all parts of our personhood and must relate in healthy ways to everything else. My fitness or unfitness impacts everyone else and their state of fitness. In pastoral ministry, this means my fitness or unfitness has a distinct relationship to my effectiveness as a pastor.

The overarching issue in congruency is how my state of fitness or unfitness relates to God's purposes. And since all of this now includes other persons and relationships, the understanding of God's purposes must include each person's understanding of God and God's purposes, and our shared stewardship.

The impact of pastoral fitness and unfitness on ministry and the future of the church is a major reason for writing this book. And it is the primary reason for efforts to promote a clergy fitness initiative across the United States. *Can you imagine the positive impact of healthier, totally fit pastors?* This joyous vision is really a possibility! And it can happen as quickly as you begin your fitness quest and encourage and support colleagues in joining this fitness initiative.

SUMMARY

In order to make the definitions and concepts of fitness presented in this chapter personal, each of you must think about how they apply to *your* body-mind-spirit fitness. It is only your fitness when it happens in *your* body, mind, and spirit. And since no one can make you fit, you have the privilege and responsibility of doing fitness for yourself, in the pursuit of God's purposes for you.

The Fitness Worksheet, on pages 173–175, is an inventory of your fitness history and potential. Please take time now to fill it out thoughtfully. Then in chapters 4, 5, and 6 you will explore your individual body, mind, and spirit in order to learn how they function, what they need, and what fitness is for each and all together.

4

Healing for Fitness

We all need healing from something.
Anonymous

Healing is one of the most comforting concepts in the English language. It means that we need not live with raw, unabated anguish and suffering. It reminds us that, although we live in a world and a human condition where sickness, mental manipulations and disorders, sin, and evil are continuous realities, our Creator has provided for shalom: salvation, peace, wholeness. Everyone needs healing from something and for something. Even thinking about healing can be healing. In this chapter I encourage everyone to be open to whatever healings we need as antecedents and support for our fitness quest.

Healing is part of salvation, shalom. Inner peace comes with healing. Outer peace comes with healing. The kingdom of God will be the completion of healing (Mal. 4:2, Rev. 22:2). But for now, for us, healing is partial, yet it can be continuous—shalom. This is also part of fitness.

Why is the church so afraid of healing? For some reason we have separated physical, mental, and spiritual healing from salvation. Perhaps we have decided that physical healing is the domain of physicians, mental and emotional healing is the sphere of psychologists, and spirituality, the part that is left over, probably is our turf. Maybe we are not sure we can compete with other healers. And we may be afraid that if we start to preach, teach, and practice healing, we will attract unattractive people into our congregations, or cause more conflict, or even go off the deep end ourselves.

We can do better than this.

I believe we are beginning to see our need for spiritual healing as a context for all other healing. We are sensing the spiritual yearnings of society as people realize they have spiritual illnesses and seek healing beyond traditional medicine and psychology. We have an opportunity to point the way toward wholeness

Since human life is flawed, and there are negative forces as well as positive forces influencing us, illnesses and disorders are not only common, they are continuous and inevitable. Moreover, human life is so complicated that we are all likely to be carrying some kinds of pathogens, wounds, and conditions of deterioration around within ourselves without paying much attention to them. Sometimes we are unaware of how sick or wounded we are until there is a crisis. For example, someone harbors several low-grade infections but is unaware until antibiotics or change to a more healthful lifestyle gives new energy, strength, and well-being. Or someone lives with sexual harassment for years and does not realize the mentally debilitating consequences until the perpetrating boss dies or moves.

The population explosion is producing signs of illness in all of us. There are now far more human beings on this planet than our infrastructures, ecological systems, and knowledge can manage healthfully. Yet many of us expect to live in the choicest locations, get whatever we want, and be rescued from the negative consequences of our lifestyles. We wound, infect, and manipulate each other in our competitions and disrespectful self-centeredness. Moreover, we are born into a world where there is barely a sustainable balance between the forces of good and the forces of evil. Such conditions produce anxiety at subconscious levels, generate pollution, and encourage risky behavior. For example, laboratory studies continue to show dangerous consequences when some kinds of animals are forced to live in crowded conditions. It is instructive to extrapolate from these findings to our human situation. Moreover, long exposure to toxins, evil, and anxieties erode natural safety buffers, as in exposure to carcinogens, oppression, and stress.

We are discovering the sickening consequences of overabundance and indulgence. On the one hand we can satiate nearly any appetite—healthy or unhealthy. On the other hand, as we live more stressful lives, we resort to unhealthy as well as healthy coping devices. Our "feel-good" attitudes move us farther and farther from practicing common-sense limitations on what we consume. A common result is the overwhelming of our natural capacities to purge excesses. For example, we smile at kids who overdose on sugar after collecting and eating excesses of Halloween candy. But we may deny the presence of similar consequences when we overeat, overintoxicate, oversleep, and submit ourselves to daily excesses. We even come to regard hectic, indulgent, compensating living as normal, forgetting the value of moderation and simplicity. Such sicknesses and wounds are not a natural part of God's creation. They are ways we make ourselves sick. For example, the Garden of Eden contained abundant food, but our metaphorical forebears chose to indulge themselves beyond healthful limits and became "sick." Our present-day indulgences perpetuate this mistake.

By now most of us have heard warnings that some pathogenic organisms adapt to our scientific efforts to control or eliminate them. This is a powerful metaphor for human efforts to control and indulge beyond natural limits and then seek to avoid natural consequences of unhealthful behavior. Excessive consumerism and an attitude of entitlement have infected us and now produce demands and consequences that strain the equilibrium of our planet and human capacities to absorb and manage noxious agents. For example, we produce deadlier guns and bigger jails to control criminals, while the criminals find more powerful weapons and spawn more inventive villainy; we invent antacids to alleviate acid reflux, then escalate our overindulgence until more serious damage is done to our digestive tracts; we take antibiotics for manageable, avoidable infections, which induces pathogens to metamorphose into more resistant, deadly agents.

Given these conditions and attitudes, we need healing from our expectations, as well as from our sicknesses and the consequences of indulgent lifestyles. We expect comfort above all and are willing to pay high prices for it. Comfort is not bad in itself, but obsessive and irresponsible demands for it leave us with serious though unrecognized mental and spiritual malaise. For example, assuaging physical-mental pain plus finding sensual pleasures in excessive medications, alcohol, recreational drugs, sugar, nicotine, caffeine, false panaceas, exercise of power and control, and so on lead to addictions beyond original need and intent.

Are you discouraged yet? These sickness and unfitness scenarios are really this serious. When we focus on them for long, they can dishearten us. In the real world, of course, we have both yin and yang, each part of the whole. Facing what is negative helps us understand what is positive.

I hope you have noted by now that healing, which we all imagine we understand, is far more complicated than is popularly assumed. This is why we must examine healing in such detail when our goal is to understand and achieve fitness. We must raise our consciousness of how sick (unfit) we can become and how complicated and involved healing and achieving fitness can be. For when we understand ourselves as more than a body and brain, we must expand our understanding of pathogens and sickness to include the mental, emotional, and spiritual dimensions of our condition. Further, if we try to become fit without healing our debilitating and contagious conditions, our fitness will be an illusion.

I have been asked if God heals us from the consequences of our unhealthy behavior. This interesting question allows us to bring formal theology and everyday beliefs into focus. Apply your theology to this question as I share my perspective.

My theology indicates that God does heal us from our sicknesses and wounds, first of all by having built into us a natural healing process that proceeds if we do not interfere with it. Second, I believe God's grace, the healing salve of God's love, supports and guides us in healing. Third, I believe that God on occasion, according to God's purposes, intervenes with miraculous healing, typically in response to intercessory (energized, focused) prayer.

My own experience indicates that healing usually occurs as a normal bodily, mental, and spiritual process, if neither outside factors nor my contrary behavior interferes. I have found that in the case of life-threatening illness or injury, healing can be facilitated by such means as prayer, positive mental attitudes, supportive relationships, medication, surgery, and my immune system. I have also found healing to be in some ways mysterious. While we can explain clotting, granulation, and other physical healing components, and we know something of psychotherapeutic assistance for the mind and spiritual healing rituals for the spirit, we do not understand fully the interrelationships of grace and human interactions, nor the dynamics of the life force that enlivens and transforms us. But we can trust these to be available in some measure to those who open themselves to God's healing processes. It seems logical to conclude that a fit body-mind-spirit will be more responsive to God's healing than an unfit body-mind-spirit.

We should note here that God's healing processes may be transforming as well as restorative. Since God's thoughts and ways are higher than ours, and since healing is in some fashion part of God's relationship with us, we may expect that transformation will be a part of healing. Such transformation may or may not fit our expectations for healing. For example, when we do not heal the way we want, this may be an opportunity for transforming our expectations of healing to conform more closely to God's purposes. There may be another kind of healing taking place through which we can learn to blend better with God's purposes for us, for those around us, for all of creation. God's process of healing may often usher us beyond recovery into significant growth. For as we contemplate the disease or injury from which we are healing, we may see how to manage our health better and discover new ways to grow and serve. We may have to live with partial healings and chronic maladies and disabilities. These are special, if difficult, challenges for body-mind-spirit fitness. Transformation is an amazing part of God's healing. We all must learn sometime that God's healing may mean transformation instead of getting what we want.

Let us note here that, while the human immune system functions autonomically and participates in both prevention and healing, the immune system itself sometimes needs healing. Immune systems may have genetic defects or become disordered through injury or serious disease, but their normal, continuous function is to deal with pathogens. Body-mind-spirit fitness has a positive effect on the immune system, and it in turn functions best in a fit body-mind-spirit. We know that we have physical immune systems, but we may need reminding that we have mental and spiritual immune systems as well. Our mental immune system is not as clearly delimited as the physical one, but it contains such active components as logic, common sense, insight, and judgment, all of which are essentially learned constituents. Then there are essentially unlearned elements such as intuition, archetypes (Carl Jung's version of the tribal and universal wisdom built into us at subconscious levels), memory, and ego (Sigmund Freud's version of strength of character). Our spiritual immune system includes such elements as conscience (partially learned and partially conditioned), discernment (a spiritual gift enhanced by spiritual disciplines), *imago Dei* (according to some theological traditions this is the seat of our relationship to God), and the guidance and support of a healthy community of faith. All of these protect us from physical, mental, and spiritual pathogens, unless we interfere with their ways of protecting, guiding, and helping us heal.

Healing makes body-mind-spirit fitness possible, and fitness facilitates healing. The peace, joy, and wholeness of healing are constantly available. The church and its spiritual leaders have been agents of healing for centuries, and still can be today. Thanks be to God! But we who are called to preach, teach, and witness to this healing must first find it for ourselves.

IMPORTANT DEFINITIONS

I devote space here to definitions and clarifications because of popular misconceptions, our tendency toward denial, and plain old forgetting of significant factors regarding health, healing, and fitness. Fitness is such a basic yet precarious dynamic that we must not assume an easy achievement of this wonderful state of being.

Healing is the recovery of a previous or higher level of health and wholeness, with the goal of blending with God's purposes. It is a natural and automatic process that will occur if it is not interfered with. Yet healing can under some conditions occur in such a way as to produce unhealthful results. Take, for instance, a fracture of a leg. If the leg is not set properly, a healed but crooked leg can result. Moreover, healing leaves scars and new strengths. The scars may be visible bodily marks, phobias, compensating habits, memories, doubts. But if understood and managed healthfully, the side effects of healing can become strengths and facilitate new levels of fitness.

Healing is God's provision of salvation in many forms for the people of God who live in a good world, but a world in which human limitations allow for and even induce sickness, injury, and unfitness. By learning fitness we participate in a continual healing and growth process in which God's purposes are our chief aim and joy.

Agency is important in healing—these agents can range from our body's healing tendencies to God's grace and innumerable human agents; from medications to patience, trust, mental images, planning, and spiritual regimens. A healing agent can be something as simple as "reframing," which is a mental process encouraged in the psychotherapeutic process called neuro-linguistic programming. In reframing we change the words we use to describe a situation so we may see it in a more helpful perspective. For example, if I were to become seriously ill, I could ask, "Why is this happening to me?" or I could ask, "What can I learn from this illness?" The first question predisposes me toward anxiety and blame, although it may help me to realize how I set myself up to be sick. The second question offers a less anxious opportunity to look for useful information.

You can use this second question right now to learn about sicknesses and recoveries in your own life. Take some time to list any serious illnesses and injuries you have had. After writing each one, add comments about what you learned from that experience. Ask yourself such questions as, What were possible causes for this experience? What aspects of this experience were negative? Which were positive? What can I do to prevent this in the future? What did this teach me about my own healing?

Crisis and sickness make headlines and sell snake oil. But our body-mind-spirit fitness vision of healing and health and our hope and trust in God's grace and purposes make healing, health, and fitness the joyful response of the people of God to a world obsessed with millennial crises, anxieties over illness, and fears of the unknown.

Jesus Christ, who devoted at least one-third of his ministry to healing, used a variety of agents: touch, exorcism prayers, saliva and dirt, exhortation. It is not the agents that produce full healing. They are symbols, cues, facilitators that open us to the process and teach us about it.

Healing also contains prophylactic elements. It reminds us to be wiser in self-management in order to avoid sickness, injury, and disorder again. Being healed allows us to focus our attention and energy on the practice of intentional high-level health. Being healed encourages us to rejoice in and be thankful for God's restorative graces. And being healed reminds us to become witnesses in the midst of sickness, wounds, and disorders of all kinds.

Wholeness is the spiritual context for healing, health, and fitness. Think of the biblical understanding of peace, wholeness, and salvation. The Hebrew term *shalom* has come into popular use to refer something similar, but shalom is an enormous, grace-filled concept, far beyond our myopic, parochial, and self-centered understandings. The term "wholeness" fits better here for the purposes of understanding healing. I believe there are five principles of wholeness, which are derived from biblical teachings.

1. Wholeness is unifying and functional. That is, wholeness is about unified beings—body, mind, and spirit. We err when we strive for wholeness in only one part of ourselves. Wholeness is a dynamic condition, the objective of which is to blend with God's purposes. It is not an end in itself, even though it is God's intention for all of creation.

2. Wholeness builds upon a requisite spiritual health process. That is, spirituality is the context for wholeness. This does not mean that wholeness is ethereal, incomprehensible, and illusionary. It means that wholeness is not divisible, and not within human control, except as we participate and facilitate. Even physicians, psychiatrists, and scientists are beginning to discuss and explore spirituality as the context for all things—a refreshing and instructive shift from the materialism and scientism of the recent past. Now, we who are called to be spiritual leaders must take spirituality and spiritual experience seriously again and teach it in ways that make sense in a materialistic, technological environment. Wholeness is different from the medical, psychological, and popular models of health and happiness (more on this later).

3. Wholeness is corporate—inclusive. We can't be whole alone. The population explosion and the interdependence and interaction of the geofamily are reminders that we cannot control and hoard God,

health resources, and wholeness for ourselves. Nor can we experience wholeness in isolation. Self-righteousness, smugness, selfishness, parochialism, and arrogance are antithetical to wholeness. But the great joy of shared wholeness is that health is as contagious as sickness. The synergy of increasing numbers of persons participating intentionally in wholeness can move us all toward health. In the largest sense, and in ways we don't understand, all peoples and all of creation share wholeness in some manner. For we believe God is moving all creation toward wholeness (Rom. 8:19–25).

4. Wholeness is not perfection. Wholeness is a process of healing and growth that includes the realities of human life. It is not just a dream or illusion of rightness and infinite excellence, it is our intentional participation in God's healing and growth process, which is offered to all. Wholeness includes our disorders, disabilities, pain, and sins, not to indulge them but to provide caring support that respects us. We can participate in wholeness even on our bad days, even in our mistakes and sins. For when we accept God's offer to participate in wholeness, we come as we are, but with grace-filled and shared possibilities.

5. Wholeness is transforming. It is dynamic in positive ways. Wholeness is not artificial or contrived change for the sake of change. Nor is it the natural changes of seasons, cycles, and stages. In the biblical sense wholeness includes possibilities for deep and comprehensive conversion from one state into a superior one that is more oriented toward God's purposes. The idea of transformation is somewhat frightening and confusing, for it can imply constant, overwhelming, out-of-control change, morphing into something unknown. But the transformations of wholeness are trustworthy, and even somewhat understandable, for they are based in God's grace. When we participate in wholeness we can discern when we need transformation, and when it is occurring. Spiritual leaders can even function as agents of wholeness and its transformations. This, of course, is one of the great joys of pastoring.

When we stop to define and understand the magnificent process of healing, it seems remarkable that the church is not more intentional in studying and facilitating it. Healing can begin with simple, intentional prayers that align us with God's healing purposes. Then healing is natural.

(Note: For another view of wholeness in contemporary perspective, see Howard Clinebell's fine book, *Well Being* (see bibliography). He prefers the term "well being" to "wholeness." He too urges self-responsibility in opening ourselves to enrichment of life.)

MODELS OF HEALING

For understanding healing, a brief review of major models of healing is useful. Five models dominate discussion today: (1) the medical model; (2) the alternative medicine model; (3) the psychological model; (4) the American dream model; and (5) the theological-spiritual model. I list them, below, with numbered steps indicating progress from the first encounter with the malady to improvement or healing.

MEDICAL MODEL

1. Diagnose (explore symptoms and name the malady).
2. Remove pathogens and irritants (eliminate what interferes with healing).
3. Medicate or intervene with a surgical procedure (prescription or surgery).
4. Monitor recovery (check on progress or deterioration).
5. Encourage prevention (advise prophylaxis).

The medical model is valuable, but it has become enslaved to a mechanistic, dualistic view of human beings and healing. Its emphasis on intervention and manipulation provide only a limited perspective on health. The medical model of health is literally the absence of illness, disabilities, and pathogens. Though this model has produced the finest medical system in the world, the American medical model has often sacrificed wholeness, alternative medicine, and spirituality to the god of science.

Even with all its limitations, traditional medicine has made progress in managing pain. It took a lot of human suffering and organized complaints about poor pain management to achieve this reform. But now traditional medicine has joined the battle against pain through use of more and better pain-relievers, by training medical personnel in more sensitive therapies, and by establishing pain clinics that deal specifically with intense and chronic pain. These models may be helpful to mental health and religious professionals for improving methods of dealing with mental and spiritual pain.

Traditional medicine has taught us the remarkable realities of the placebo effect, via research in which medication is given to some people and a neutral substance to others, no one knowing which they are taking. Healing may occur in some who take neutral substances as a result of the patient's belief in the efficaciousness of healer and substance. So caring attention, administration of some substance or ritual, plus belief by the recipient can produce healing effects.

Traditional medicine has also helped bring in the age of Prozac, as a growing number of psychotropic pharmaceuticals are used to alter brain and other organic functions. Mood changes, emotional overloads, and mental disorders can now be modified by chemical interventions.

ALTERNATIVE MEDICINE MODEL

1. Listen to the body's signals (seek signs of the body's functioning).
2. Use touch (massage, acupressure, acupuncture, energizing), herbs, and medications to support the body's healing efforts.
3. Aid body and mind in working together (coordinate thinking and therapy).
4. Encourage lifestyle changes that facilitate health.

Traditional Western medicine is beginning to accept alternative treatments and therapies, such as homeopathic and osteopathic medicine, herbal medicine, chiropractic, acupuncture, massage, and even the work of shamans. The American public has pushed traditional medical practitioners to include any demonstrably helpful practices into a partnership for healing.

Alternative medicine has emphasized eating (or not eating) for purposes of healing and health. Some practitioners even declare that food can be medicine. Through such insights we are learning that food is for both nutrition and healing.

I include the role of shaman (ancient and contemporary versions) in alternative medicine because throughout history the shaman has tended to demonstrate the value of symbols, rituals, cues, and art forms in facilitating healing. As with the placebo effect, belief on the part of the recipient aids this process, as it does in all forms of healing.

Not long ago I attended the Harvard Medical School's second Conference on Spirituality and Healing in Medicine in Los Angeles, an enormously stimulating event. For three days several thousand medical professionals and a handful of us theological types listened to presentations on various healing models from around the world, and from both medical and theological perspectives. Especially valuable for me were the research presentations that identified at least 150 scientifically controlled studies that indicate the significant, positive difference religious faith makes in physical healing, from disease and surgical procedures.

Numerous well-known psychiatrists have called for dialogue and cooperation between medicine and theology, including such authorities as Carl Jung, Paul Tournier, Karl Menninger, M. Scott Peck, Gerald May, Herbert Benson, Dale Matthews, and Larry Dossey. How odd that these psychiatrists speak with assurance about the role of religious faith in healing and health, yet many pastors and theologians are unsure of our role in healing and health. Many major medical schools in the United States now include at least one course in spirituality, healing, and health, but I know of only a handful of seminaries that have a course in healing or encourage active dialogue between medical, psychotherapeutic, and theological professionals. Thank God for medical leadership in spirituality and healing, but we religious professionals can do our part much better than we are at present.

PSYCHOLOGICAL MODEL

1. Assess complaints and basic mental condition (note characteristics, history).
2. Offer or select therapeutic options (discuss possibilities).
3. Provide psychotherapy (begin selected treatment).
4. Encourage healthy mental health practices (advise for learning/maturity).

The psychological model of health and healing is still relatively new, compared to the medical model. But it is based on the medical model, and many of its practitioners are medically trained. One of its greatest benefits has been the birth of pop psychology. Pop psychology, even with its excesses and spawning of misconceptions, has encouraged Americans to pay attention to their thinking and the process of socialization. Many people have learned how to take charge of their thinking and, with professional guidance, to change maladaptive cognitive and affective behavior. This model limits itself to the functioning of the mind, however, and though it talks of holistic perspectives, it seldom takes spirituality seriously. Fortunately, the pastoral counseling and chaplaincy professions have begun to influence psychology, even though psychological theory and methods dominated their early formations. Presently they are bridging the gap between psychological and theological understandings of mental-spiritual processes.

The American Dream Model

1. Work hard (do your best).
2. Live right (be moral, kind, responsible).
3. Reap the just rewards of such living (health, happiness, security).
4. If necessary, sacrifice personal interests for group benefit.

The society produced by this model has been the envy of much of the nondemocratic world. Its vulnerabilities have become apparent, however: consumerism, entitlement thinking, and manipulative thinking. There is no specific prescription for healing in the American dream, other than moving to another location, trying harder, changing jobs, simply coping until retirement, and trusting physicians.

The Theological-Spiritual Model

1. Discern sickness (use prayer, confession, theology, history).
2. Encourage hope, belief, and right living (teach spiritual/mental health).
3. Connect with God and the community of faith (build relationships).
4. Administer symbolic and reinforcing rituals (prayers, anointing, Eucharist).
5. Develop a healthy environment (promote wholeness in life/family/work).
6. Celebrate, worship, and serve (recognize sources of healing; praise God).
7. Avoid pseudo-healing: self-righteousness, denial, comfort (be realistic).

The spiritual model also has limitations and excesses, yet for some years now it has encouraged a trend toward wholeness based on spirituality. Its model of healing is based on the shalom understanding of salvation, forgiveness, love, and prayer. Unfortunately, organized religion has tended to neglect the teaching and practice of healing. Perhaps the church is on the verge of recovering this aspect of its ministry.

All of these models of healing have something to commend them. All have contributed to constructive understandings of healing, as well as to misconceptions.

LEVELS AND STAGES OF HEALING

Healing doesn't occur in a vacuum. It occurs most reliably when all parties understand as much as possible about the condition and its remedies. However, physical-mental-spiritual mysteries are involved. That is where trust in an agent of healing and in God as the source come into play. With the enormous increase in scientific knowledge, improvement in therapies, and increase in self-knowledge, contemporary communities and individuals can participate in healing with greater competence. We are also becoming more realistic about the relativity of healing, the presence of chronic conditions that can be managed but perhaps not healed, and the actual mechanics of recovery. The following discussion of levels of healing reviews some contemporary perspectives on the progression of a healing process. This list is not necessarily hierarchical nor is every stage inevitable.

Level 1: Healing as recovery. Here we open our consciousness to the realities of our physical, mental, and spiritual sicknesses and disorders. At this level we are engrossed in the discomfort and decision making of healing. Here we wrestle with pain, medications, anger, frustration, confusion, hope, trust, and the choices of how to handle the healing process.

Level 2: Healing as learning. At this level we begin to learn about our sick self and well self. We learn what works and what doesn't work. We learn about prophylaxis and the value of fitness, if we are on a fitness quest. And we sometimes learn how much we yet need to learn and practice.

Level 3: Healing as a shared condition. We are sick, disordered, and unfit together. Therefore, the healing we seek is also a shared condition. Earlier, when the principles of biblical wholeness were discussed, we noted that wholeness is corporate. And now we see that sickness is corporate: although only a specific person or persons may have a particular illness, we are all affected by contagion, costs, and remedies. It should follow that recovery and learning are also sharing processes. Further, the fitness discussed in this book is a shared process. Think about it.

Level 4: Healing as stewardship—of personhood, the community of faith, and creation. Since the Fall all of creation has been sick, disordered, unfit in some basic ways. Everyone participates individually and in shared ways. Therefore, when we seek, open ourselves to, and learn healing, we share in the largest dimension of healing.

You know by now that I do not look at fitness through rose-colored glasses, nor offer happy-go-lucky panaceas. "Life is difficult," said M. Scott Peck in the opening words of his book *The Road Less Traveled,* in which he discussed the human struggle to make life bearable and worthwhile. But we are not without peaceful and joyful messages about healing and fitness.

Do you remember the positive and wholesome outcomes in two out of the three cases I cited at the beginning of this book? These outcomes were the result of healing. It may be useful here to go back and reread those cases, and then answer the following questions:

1. What were the healing ingredients in each case?
2. How did healing occur?
3. What blocked full healing in the John Jenkins case?
4. How would you have facilitated healing if you had been the pastoral counselor?

THE FORGIVENESS FORMULA AS HEALING AGENT

A prime example of a spiritual healing agent is found in what we can call the forgiveness formula. It is a distillation of familiar theological and biblical traditions. There are other healing agents, of course: liturgy, Eucharist, anointing, prayer, and such. And you are encouraged to bring your own tradition, experience, and theology to this reading of the exceptionally valuable healing process of forgiveness. But the forgiveness formula is receiving much attention in secular as well as religious circles these days, and therefore offers a broad range of data and experience concerning the effects of spiritual healing on mind and body, as well as spirit. It is a particularly useful formula here, for it delineates concrete stages of the healing that occurs through participating in forgiveness.

Step 1: Hearing the gospel. This is the starting place for forgiveness. The gospel makes it clear that all are sinners (Rom. 3:23). The gospel has no place for those who believe other people are sinners, but they themselves are not, or are not as bad. Recognizing that we are all (including me) sinners helps us begin the forgiveness process on equal footing before God and with each other. This can be quite uncomfortable for someone who suffers from grievous injury and injustice. But human history makes it clear that unless we recognize the leveling effect of the gospel declaration, we cannot be freed from endless cycles of vengeance, anger, and fear. We are all prone to error, intentionally and unintentionally. We are all participants in evil and sin in some way. Therefore we all begin with a need to be forgiven, and with opportunities to enact God's forgiveness as a way of healing our own wounds.

An incredible example of forgiveness in action was enacted in the Truth and Reconciliation Commission, led by Archbishop Desmond Tutu, in South Africa. This commission offered opportunities for people who had perpetrated murder and other crimes during apartheid to confess this publicly, and thereby be immune from criminal charges. In its public hearings the commission allowed the family members of persons abused and slain to come witness the perpetrators as they confessed. Then they were encouraged to forgive the perpetrators in order that they and the country, and even the perpetrators, might be healed and freed from the urge to seek vengeance. In Northern Ireland, Bosnia, the Mideast, and many other places, ordinary people are trying to learn how to interdict the egregious cycles of vengeance that do not allow forgiveness to heal human wounds. The gospel of Jesus Christ begins with hearing and understanding that all are indicted under the laws of God, no matter the excuses.

Step 2: Confessing our sin. We confess our culpability and vulnerability to and with each other in order to be saved from the guilt of our sins (1 John 1:9). This helps free us from projecting blame on others, even when they have harmed us. And it helps us begin with the one factor we control—ourselves. When I confess my sin sincerely, it is not as easy to accuse others. This confessing of my own sin is also my witness and model of willingness to participate in forgiveness instead of vengeance, no matter the vulnerability.

Step 3: Accepting forgiveness from God, each other, and creation. We do not invent forgiveness, we can only reproduce it, according to God's model and that of Jesus Christ (Matt. 6:12; Eph. 4:32). Forgiveness becomes our practice of the kingdom of God. We join God in forgiving our enemies and the perpetrators of our abuse, whether they seek our forgiveness or not. For thereby we acknowledge that we cannot live healthy (fit) lives while retaining the toxin of unforgiveness.

Forgiveness does not come cheap. But its benefits are priceless. Under the discipline of forgiveness, we forgive whether we feel like it or not, whether it is deserved or not, and by stages if not immediately. We can do this because God, creation, and the *imago Dei* within give us at least a minimal pool of goodwill to tap, and because we tap into the forgiveness of God, which is already operative and healing. We can do this because of the enormous reservoir of awareness developed in our society by the sense of fairness the American Constitution promotes, the spiritual awareness nineteenth-century revivalists generated, and the sense of interdependency that is replacing rugged individualism. We also have the lessons of the behavioral sciences and theology, and the dedicated practice of pastors, pastoral psychotherapists, mental health professionals, and medical practitioners. Together we have raised the national consciousness regarding human need, the urgency of this need, and the resources available to meet that need.

Step 4: Doing penance (Luke 3:8; Acts 26:20). Doing penance reminds us of the pain and cost of error and evil. It is not enough to offer and receive the words of forgiveness. We must make real and symbolic restitution, and stop the hurtful practices. For even though the abuse cannot be rescinded, nor the damage fully repaired, penance offers trustworthy demonstration of repentance and the probability that this sin will not be repeated, at least not easily. It is important in this stage for those on whom pain and damage have been inflicted to participate in defining needed penance.

At this fourth step a painful and critical separation occurs between repentant sinners and unrepentant sinners, and between those who forgive as they receive real or symbolic restitution and those who must forgive without repentance or restitution on the part of their abuser. For the latter, a great step of faith in the healing power of God's forgiveness process is required, for not only must the grievance be endured, but the lack of repentance and restitution is an added burden.

This heavy load is crushing unless it is laid down, let go, through God's applied grace and our appropriation of that grace.

Step 5: Pronouncing absolution (John 20:23; 2 Cor. 2:5–11). This is a declaration of the termination of suffering caused by sin. It is not denial. It is not a fantasy that memories of the abuse and pain will disappear. The sin was real, but so was the forgiveness. The memories will not disappear but they can be healed. The pain will become a manageable scar. The urges for retribution, the victim attitude, will fade when someone in authority (priest or pastor), or all of us together pronounce absolution in Jesus' name. Our model, of course, is Jesus Christ, who, while suffering on the cross, said, "It is finished!" (John 19:30). This means the end of accusations, discussion, or obsession about the abuse. Thereby we open ourselves to the healing that can only occur through forgiveness and absolution. We can even open ourselves to the healing in partial or postponed healing. For God's grace completes what we cannot.

An understanding of healing as more than physical recovery shows that healing, in its broader meanings, can be extended beyond the physical to include attitudes, relationships, memories, counterproductive schedules, habits, lifestyles, congregations, spiritual malaise that does not need repentance, and such. This book offers an opportunity for all of us to assess, heal, and transform constricted understandings of salvation, wholeness, healing, health, fitness, stewardship, ministry, and God's purposes.

Pain is a special case for healing. For pain is more than a bodily discomfort, it is a distress signal that involves body, mind, and spirit. We all know about physical pain, for we all experience it and talk about it. We also know something about mental anguish (pain), but we don't understand and talk about this as readily. Spiritual despair (pain) is even less understood and discussed. Yet in each experience where pain exists, body, mind, and spirit converge. This means that as we open ourselves to seek to facilitate healing, we need to involve body, mind, and spirit. The natural response to severe or continuous bodily pain is to pray that it be taken away. Yet the mental component of pain may remain unattended. Therefore in body-mind-spirit fitness, healing involves concern for healing the bodily experience of pain, along with the mental and spiritual pain.

In recent years pain clinics have aided patients who must deal with chronic pain by offering training as well as medication for living with pain. These clinics take the mental part of the process seriously, such as by suggesting that patients learn to "relax into your pain." Various relaxation techniques are used to assist this process. Then patients learn to reframe the way they think about themselves and their pain, until the pain is simply a manageable part of their lives. Adding the spiritual healing dynamic, not only do we pray to God for the removal of pain and its causes, we accept grace to assuage the mental anguish and the spiritual despair so that we may even become thankful for the part pain plays in life.

The apostle Paul's notable experience with bodily, mental, and spiritual pain, described in 2 Corinthians 12:1–10, is an enlightening perspective on his struggle with what was probably some kind of persistent and troubling physical malady. As he prays, he learns the lesson that "my grace is sufficient for you," in which he becomes "content" with the overriding power of Christ in his life, even when there is pain. This is an example, not of denial nor escapism, but rather of learning and living in God's "higher thoughts and higher ways" (Isa. 55:9).

In chapters that follow I will discuss many other ingredients of healing, for the ingredients of health and fitness are also constituents of healing. Nutrition, breathing, exercise, attitude, relaxation, meditation, caring, and stewardship are vitally important resources of healing. Be prepared to incorporate these insights about healing into your fitness quest.

SUMMARY

It may be helpful now to use the ABCs outline (chapter 3) to review healing as discussed in this chapter. A successful fitness quest is impossible if you are not participating in a healing process, for healing frees you from the baggage and toxins that negate health and fitness.

A–Awareness: Healing is necessary for body-mind-spirit fitness.
  Healing is part of biblical wholeness (shalom).
  We can blend secular and religious healing models.
  There is interrelationship between physical, mental, and
    spiritual healing.
  There are progressive levels of healing.

B–Basics: The forgiveness formula is a primary resource and
  model for healing.

C–Congruency: Healing is a function of union-communion with God.

Healing is important for all of our relationships, for it brings reconciliation, reconstruction, respect, and new insights.

In the next chapter I focus on body fitness. Learning good stewardship of the body helps us understand good stewardship of mind and spirit—the total self.

5

Bodily Fitness

> Do you not know that your body is a temple of the Holy Spirit within you, . . . and that you are not your own? For you were bought with a price; therefore glorify God in your body.
>
> *1 Corinthians 6:19–20*

Feeling healthy and strong is about as fine a feeling as we can have. No one feels this way all the time. But anyone can increase that "being the best that I can be" feeling. This is the physical experience we are aiming for in this chapter. For it is available to all of us, no matter what our physical state is.

"Being the best that I can be" is such a deeply satisfying and useful state that it is worth working for, and in this chapter I offer realistic, dependable guidance for achieving and maintaining that condition. Physical fitness is part of our fitness quest.

As you begin the actual lived process of the fitness quest, remind yourself of the body-mind-spirit unity and connections. For though the focus is now on bodily functions, we are still dealing with full personhood—a whole human being. State the connectedness specifically. You can state this in your words and ideas; I state it as follows.

THE MENTAL CONNECTION

Our brains-hearts-bodies are hardwired. But that I mean that (1) the body affects and functions at the direction of the mind, and (2) the mind is directly affected by the body in which it lives. Mental health tends to induce physical health, and physical health tends to induce mental health. Mental and physical disorders and illnesses have the opposite effects. In the largest sense, our bodies cannot be fully fit if our minds are not fit. In everyday living, of course, our bodies can be in pretty good shape even when our minds are not functioning well, just as our minds can function well even when our bodies are sick, injured, disabled, or tired. But the connection and influence remain. I will discuss the spiritual connection and recall the interconnections of all three again later.

This rational connection occurs at both unconscious and conscious levels. Sigmund Freud gave us a great gift by emphasizing the mind-body connection and by demonstrating the influence the unconscious mind has on the body and human behavior. At the unconscious level our training, experience, and habits determine our thinking and behavior now unless we alter this pre-programmed connection by making conscious choices to act and think differently. We do this regularly as we grow up and mature, of course. But mature adults begin to realize that we can make such conscious choices continually, and we must make them if we are to continue appropriate development.

Now you are making a conscious choice about body-mind-spirit fitness: Will you begin, or continue, a fitness quest? For most Americans, unfitness is the attitude of choice, even if we do not realize we've made the choice. Some choose one part of fitness by aiming for high mental fitness or strong physical fitness, and a few aim for deep spiritual fitness. This book encourages your fitness quest toward total fitness.

If you choose to remain unfit, this choice and condition will continue your unfitness of body, mind, and spirit and will occasion further deterioration. If you choose fitness and continue to make the small choices that facilitate fitness, you will experience better health and the other benefits of body-mind-spirit fitness. You will never arrive at perfection, of course; but you will occasion further growth. This conscious, rational choice to be fit turns out, then, to be a most significant choice. Fitness, after all, is a choice, an attitude, a pilgrimage, rather than a static condition. It is literally a commitment, a covenant with yourself and with God. By beginning a fitness quest, you are already participating in fitness and making it easier and easier to continue on into a fitness lifestyle. When you say, I choose fitness, the benefits are enormous!

THE SPIRITUAL CONNECTION

Our bodies-hearts-spirits are, in contrast, soft-wired. The connections are not as tangible and noticeable as the physical connections, but they are just as real. The spiritual dynamic of our personhood includes connections between ourselves and that which is greater than ourselves, that larger context that we know exists and can sense in some ways. The interaction of the material world with the spiritual context is mysterious and experiential at the same time. The phenomenologists (Edmund Husserl, Maurice Merleau-Ponty, for example) tried to give us a rational way to understand this connection. But for most of us the body-mind-spirit connections must be experienced and learned through interactions with the material, the mental, and the spiritual.

I note the spiritual in fitness here as a reminder that physical behavior is also spiritual, and spirituality affects behavior. The spiritual realm operates well beyond our physical limits, of course. But we participate in it, and we influence it as it influences us. In everyday experience this means that decisions about eating, exercise, and production are spiritual decisions. The spiritual dimension is discussed more fully in chapter 7.

THE PHYSICAL CONNECTION

The observations given below regarding bodily fitness suggest a perspective on this worthy yet complicated subject. As always, you should bring your own experience and perspectives to this subject. But do not be limited to your past or your present knowledge regarding bodily fitness. I hope you will be in dialogue with me through this book, and especially as we consider physical issues. For this is the most concrete model we have to work with as we explore body-mind-spirit fitness.

Body-Mind-Spirit. A physical body is only part of human personhood. Contemporary theology and the holistic movements assert that the unity of body-mind-spirit is a basic human reality. However, body, mind, and spirit are also dimensions, dynamics, or constituents of personhood that contribute identifiable characteristics to it. They are interactive and interdependent. This blend is both mysterious and tangible, as recognized in Psalm 139:14: "I am fearfully and wonderfully made."

The body is the most visible and experiential aspect of our personhood. Therefore it can function as a representation, a paradigm for understanding mind and spirit. Yet there is great danger in such extrapolation, for the body image can severely limit our understanding of mind-spirit dynamics. The mind is the brain-heart combination in which the brain promotes individuality and the heart promotes relationships. The spirit is our *imago Dei* and our spiritual consciousness.

Images. Bodies exist in two ways: the first is our actual body, and the second is the mental image we have of our body. One is reality-based, the other is fantasy. It is important to compare constantly your actual body and your fantasy body as you explore bodily fitness. Often it is difficult to distinguish between these two, for your mental image of your physical self is so powerful that it usually dominates perception unless you factor it out. This fantasy body is constructed of biases, reactions, and misconceptions. One task, then, is to clarify who you are, actually, in the physical sense. For if you do not, you may only tinker futilely with a fantasy self instead of exploring and enhancing your actual physical self.

In order to make the fitness quest effective you must get in touch with and relate mentally and spiritually to your material body. Here are some useful ways to do this:

> *Journal.* If you haven't done so already, begin writing your thoughts, new information, and experiences as you continue your fitness quest. Even if you do not like to write about yourself (there's a message in there somewhere), or do not expect to continue journaling, I encourage you to do this at least at the beginning of a fitness quest. The act of putting thoughts and experiences on paper focuses them and preserves them for review, discussion, and celebrations to come.

> Various formats can be helpful for journaling. Using the "flow-of-consciousness" format means just writing whatever comes to mind. This is useful for those who like to watch themselves think . . . spontaneously. Or you could use a structured outline for each entry, such as how you are feeling, what negative experiences and what positive experiences you are having, questions to answer, exercises to complete, dreams to articulate, unusual experiences to contemplate, and such. And, of course, you may vary your format and invent one which serves you well.

> *Mirror.* For years I had a full-length mirror on casters in my counseling office. I found it had high impact for persons who had overreacted to their fantasy self, who had an unrealistic image of themselves, or who were afraid to own their physical selves. When I felt a client needed to be in closer touch with her or his physical body, I would roll the mirror nearby as a reference point.

> Take a long, dispassionate look at your body in a full length mirror, clothed and unclothed. Jot your impressions in your journal.

Then write a few observations about those impressions. When your reactions have cooled, take time to read Psalm 139, and give thanks to God for your physical self. Then begin a dialogue with God about the stewardship of your body. Do this with gentleness, respect, and honesty. For one of the goals of the fitness quest is respect and appreciation for your bodily self, as it is now and as it will be.

Alter Ego. Remember the Johari Window exercise—drawing a square box with four compartments, comparing what we can see and not see of ourselves, and what aspects others can see and not see in us? Remember what it taught us some years ago? None of us can see and know every aspect of ourselves. Therefore, it is useful to solicit the impressions of close friends, mentors, professional consultants, and even enemies concerning your physical self. If you listen carefully you can confirm or correct your self-impressions. Having a "buddy" in the fitness quest is exceptionally valuable for support, sharing the quest, and correcting misconceptions, if you are given honest feedback.

Motivations. We are getting serious now about transforming unfit practices and lifestyles. So if you haven't already, this is the time to do a "gut check," an honest assessment of your motivations for the fitness quest. Why are you interested in a fitness quest? What energy source will you tap to overcome natural resistances, denial, boredom, fear, and everyday obstacles? Do you have a clear vision of yourself as a healing, morphing, joyous, real, live person? (Note: The reference point for the word "joy" in this book is not giddy euphoria, or even happiness. I regard joy as one of the precious emotional-spiritual feelings that accompany a fitness quest and the experience of full fitness. Finding this emotion will be one of your finest assets and motivators.)

A quotation from Kenneth H. Cooper, M.D., author of *Faith-Based Fitness,* can be helpful here. He says, "What's the secret to bridging this gap between merely wishing you were in shape and actually getting into shape? The answer begins with belief—specifically, your deepest personal convictions about what is good and true and ultimately important about your life." Here in this book we assume a strong personal faith as a resource and guide for a fitness quest. The power of belief is crucial. Belief is discussed under spiritual fitness later. In this book the word "attitude" refers to beliefs translated into a mood that guides behavior.

Energy. Energy, vitality, "elan vital" (Henri Bergson) are some generic terms for the ineffable and incredible life force that powers our universe and our individual selves. This is the primal power resource available to us, emanating from God. We experience it in physical, emotional, mental, and spiritual forms, as well as see its pervasive presence in everything around us. We do not originate such energy, but we open ourselves to it, and we manage whatever amount of it we take in as if it were ours alone. We note the synergy (energy enhanced by pooling individual energies) of groups and recognize similarities to our individual experiences of energy. An automobile engine is a metaphor for this. It does not produce its fuel, but only burns it for power. Carrying the engine metaphor further, we all know that an engine functions more efficiently when it is clean and well-maintained. Just so, a fit body-mind-spirit accesses and uses energy more efficiently than when unfit. Groups and their synergy are like parts of this engine.

Our understanding of energy is becoming more sophisticated. Quantum physics is taking over from Newtonian physics, and terms such as "fifth force" and "L-energy" are building on Albert Einstein's stunning insight that mass (matter) is a version of energy. Now we are told that information is energy. Information in this context means data, experience, and wisdom, and it is shared instantaneously and continuously among all living things. (For further information on these new concepts, see *Chaos*, by James Gleick; *The Heart's Code*, by Paul Pearsall; *The HeartMath Solution*, by Doc Childre and Howard Martin.)

As you think about this dynamic concept of energy, you will no doubt connect it with spirituality, which is our most direct connection with God. And this adds another dimension to fitness. For if body-mind-spirit fitness brings a greater capacity for, and more efficiency in, managing energy, the benefits for personal, relational, and ministry empowerment become awesome. Exciting, isn't it!?

Stewardship. "Fitness is good stewardship." This is one of the slogans that guide and inspire a fitness quest. The quest is not for one person alone; it is for the benefit of others as well. And it is one of our responsibilities under God. You are the only person to whom God has entrusted the stewardship of your body. Others share some responsibility for your health and fitness, but you are the only person in charge of your fitness quest. Awesome, isn't it?

The Bible and theology, as well as psychology, sociology, and medicine, warn of the consequences of personal and communal unfitness. Being unfit denies personal responsibility before God and denies the negative consequences for others. "Do you not know that your body is a temple of the Holy Spirit within you, which you have from God, and that you are not your own? For you were bought with a price; therefore glorify God in your body" (1 Cor. 6:19–20). This strong language is the apostle's warning that we not harm God's creations. The point of this caveat is not to induce guilt and fear, but rather to point out the joyful responsibilities we have for each other's fitness and mission, and our personal response to God's entrusted gifts. If I read the Bible correctly, it indicates continually that we were not created for indulgence and self-centeredness but for God's purposes of wholeness and mission. The Bible and the community of faith remind us of the difference between comfort and indulgence and faithful stewardship.

Resources. Many resources are available to guide and support your fitness quest. Not all are of equal value. And some purport to be true and helpful but are not. The bibliography lists resources I have found helpful. But the one book I urge everyone to purchase is *On Your Way to Fitness,* by C. Everett Koop, M.D., former U.S. Surgeon General. It is available from The Koop Foundation, P.O. Box 998, Hanover, NH, 03755-0998 and is a simple, reliable, clear guide to much of the information needed for physical fitness. And it contains the Food Guide Pyramid offered by the U.S. Department of Agriculture, which has become the reference point for healthful nutrition.

There is no shortage of research, information, theorizing, and commercials regarding physical health and fitness. Here, I offer not an exhaustive review of all of it but a selective and eclectic summary of what I have found helpful in my ministry, counseling practice, teaching, and personal life.

THE ABCS OUTLINE

This chapter, as well as the whole book, is organized around the ABC format presented earlier. The ABCs format is a helpful structure for organizing and summarizing information in order to focus on the essentials needed for a particular subject. This outline will be used throughout this book to help organize the insights and practices of body-mind-spirit fitness. Following is a summary of answers to nutritional questions in each of the categories of the ABC's acronym.

In the discussion that follows, nutrition and exercise are treated as units of bodily fitness. Each is discussed as part of the other, yet each also needs its own analysis because the subjects are different.

NUTRITION

NUTRITION AND THE ABCS

"A" Stands for Awareness

What do I know and need to know about nutritional fitness?

Some points can never be made too frequently:

1. Fitness has enormous benefits.
2. Fitness is not automatic; it is a choice.
3. Knowledge of body parts and their functions is important.
4. Each body is unique.
5. Eating is a critical factor in fitness.
6. Attitude, the openness to change, is important.
7. Openness to experience and new information is a mark of "the fully functioning person," as the psychologist Carl Rogers taught a generation ago. We need consistent reference points, but we also need an openness to the dynamics of life. The tension between what we know and what we are learning is a stimulating aspect of our fitness quest.

Of course, information is only a resource; it is not fitness itself. You can even get too much information, overwhelming yourself with too many ideas. Turning information into practice and actual fitness is the joyous transformation in which we feel fitness occurring.

"B" Stands for Basics

What basic resources and experiences determine fitness?

Attitude. Review your attitude continually lest it sabotage your fitness quest. Let your mind and spirit choose from the beliefs, values, and benefits of healthful nutrition and exercise in this book, and focus these into your own positive attitude.

Nutrition/Food/Eating. Fueling the body includes the ingestion of nutrients and the management of such nutrition. We all have nutritional illusions and misconceptions, as well as personal appetites and eating habits. Because of our incorrect ideas, I will refer regularly to important guidelines for changing counterproductive eating habits, including the Food Guide Pyramid from the U.S. Department of Agriculture.

Basic Guidelines. Some simple guidelines for changing from feeding our unfitness to feeding our fitness may help you get started.

- Eat less. This is the crux of fitness for many. Here all the "demons" are engaged, and we face the hard reality that we eat much more than we need, and we are part of a nation that overeats continually. Do we really have the wisdom and courage to eat wisely? Motivations to eat wisely are mostly negative. But the flip-side of these motivators is that fitness takes away nearly all of these negative consequences of unfitness. Positive, indeed!

    In *On Your Way to Fitness*, C. Everett Koop states, "If you eat too much—and exercise too little—you will gain weight. It's as simple as that." We will discuss exercise later, but for now we are noting some simple data about our nutritional habits. Research evidence is mounting that eating less, especially reducing calories, cuts down on the likelihood of brain disease, aids brain efficiency, and adds to a healthy lifespan. How many incentives do we need?

    Many of us know we should and could eat less to achieve fitness. We are beginning to realize that being overweight costs all of us big money, causes many to spend years being sick, and causes many to die prematurely. Americans are the fattest people on earth, except for Samoans, and we are all paying the bills for this, for we have more weight-related diseases than any other nation.

    A recent study of the baby-boomer generation, reported by the American College of Physicians-American Society of Internal Medicine, indicates that a twenty-pound weight gain since high school doubles the risk of diabetes and post-menopausal breast cancer, and more than doubles the risk of heart disease and arthritis. The time to make the lifestyle changes necessary to avoid these risks, that is, to modify diet, exercise, manage stress, and get treatment for medical problems, is between the ages of 35 and 55.

    I do not mean to attack overweight people. The issue is not about physical beauty. Rather I hope I am offering encouragement

to you to take a major step toward fitness by achieving appropriate body mass. Body mass is a popular term that has acquired a scientific meaning with the development of the "body mass index,"
a useful guide to understanding the significance of bodily weight.
If you want to calculate your BMI, multiply your weight in pounds
by 703 and divide the result by your height in inches squared (or
search "body mass index" on the Internet, which will produce a list
of sites that calculate BMI for you). The U.S. Food and Drug
Administration standards now say we should have a BMI of less
than 25 to be fit. (A BMI over 30 is classified as obese.)

- Eat one-half of what you would ordinarily eat at one sitting. If
you eat out, order less or draw an imaginary line across your
plate and either leave one-half of the food serving or take one-
half home. This provides a practical starting point and relieves
typical anxieties about giving up all the good things in order to
lose weight and be fit. If you do not wish to change the foods you
eat, at least eat less of them. Our bodies now typically use one-
third of their energy digesting the food we eat and processing
the noxious ingredients. There are clear benefits in eating less.

Starting your nutrition changes by trying to talk yourself out
of all your favorite but unhealthy foods may sabotage your fitness quest. If you find that you cannot give up chocolate, simply
eat less of it. If you cannot give up butter, eat less of it. If you
cannot give up your favorite unhealthful beverages, cut down on
them and drink more water. But if you can go all the way and
combine eating less with eating more wisely, you will advance
more quickly on your fitness quest. Choices!

Some people, however, need to eat more, or at least more of
the right foods for them. If you are malnourished, seek advice
from a nutritionist or medical doctor if you are confused or have
a condition that suggests you need medical help.

- Eat more often. Weight-loss specialists and nutritionists generally suggest that eating less but eating more often is best for
achieving an appropriate weight without too much hunger pang
anxiety. You can incorporate both eating less and eating more
often into your fitness quest.

- Eat smarter. If you want to go beyond just eating less and losing
some weight, then a study of good nutrition and food preparation
is important. My reference point here again is Dr. Koop's *On Your*

Way to Fitness. It contains the Food Guide Pyramid, which divides food into basic categories. And it suggests the number of portions daily of each food category that will be commensurate with good nutrition.

If you are one of the many Americans who do not typically eat healthfully, you will need to form new grocery shopping and food preparation habits. Habit changes are less difficult when motivation is strong, so I will assume at this stage that your motivation is still strong. Make your shopping list before going grocery shopping, and list foods and portions that support fitness eating. Prepare vegetable sticks and other healthy low-calorie snacks ahead of time, so that when you are hungry, healthful food is readily available. You will need some will power (motivation) to substitute veggie sticks, fruits, unsalted nuts, and such for sweets and junk food, but the transition will bring great rewards as you cultivate new tastes.

- Try using smaller utensils (smaller forks and spoons), taking smaller bites, pausing between bites, and chewing more slowly.
- Make your eating place more attractive and restful, play relaxing music, engage in conversation, read or journal.
- If you drink a large glass of water about fifteen minutes before eating a meal, you will feel fuller and therefore less hungry when you eat.
- Weigh yourself at the same time every day. This allows your body to give you a verifiable signal about nutrition. The scale is not an enemy; it is a friend.
- Develop a mental image of yourself as leaner and firmer. This will become a motivating goal. Remember that being thin or looking like someone else is not the goal. Rather, the goal is you in body-mind-spirit fitness.
- Have one or more partners. A friend or colleague or family member who will go on the fitness quest with you is supportive. You can laugh, cry, pray, and celebrate together. Loners will have a difficult time with a fitness quest sooner or later.
- Eat slowly; savor your food; eat thankfully.

Psychology, Biology, and Eating Patterns. Many of us worry about so-called hunger pangs, even though we have probably heard that our typical hunger pangs are not signals that we need food, but that we are bored, need habitual stress reducers, or are in a setting that cues eating fantasies. Both overweight and fit bodies have great storage capacities and large stores of potential nutrition. So it would take several days for us to actually *need* food. Of course, we would begin to experience true hunger earlier. This is one reason we will discuss fasting later. We need to know what our bodies are signaling: separating normal "hunger pangs" from signals about our nutritional needs is important.

Most of us learned the psychological value of food as infants, when we learned to seek food for comfort and attention. We felt deprived and rejected when we sought feeding and were rejected. Some of those psychological connections to food continue to the present. We comfort ourselves with food. We find attention and entertainment in food. We feel deprived when told to give up certain foods. All of these infantile associations are engaged by advertisers trying to sell us their food products. Here is where the power of the mind to sort out reality and health from fantasy and consumerism is valuable. This is why fitness and your fitness quest must be thoughtful endeavors. Spiritual disciplines add strength to rational efforts to break the immature connections between eating and comfort.

We need to understand how body chemistry contributes to hunger feelings and eating. The master control of the body's neural and chemical cues is in the brain's hypothalamus, but the biochemical cues are all over the body. For example, the neurotransmitter serotonin triggers a hunger feeling for carbohydrates. Various hormones try to maintain a balance in body chemistry. Eating the wrong foods can trigger a chain reaction that induces us to eat other inappropriate foods. Taking antacids is an example of the way we try to use chemicals to overcome unpleasant balancing reactions instead of eating less and differently to maintain a healthful balance. Such biochemical-psychological reactions commonly sabotage our best eating intentions. Therefore, the fitness quest requires us to gain an adequate knowledge of how our body functions, so that subconscious cues and reactions do not abort our sincere intentions. Some of the material listed in the bibliography can provide adequate information. But you still must add commitment to this knowledge and put it into practice. Again, remind yourself that this is worthwhile.

For many people, eating smarter requires more guidance than the Food Guide Pyramid provides. If you haven't already done so, now is the time to explore your cookbooks for attractive recipes that use healthful ingredients. Buy a low-fat or vegetarian cookbook. You don't have to become a vegetarian or an obsessive calorie-counter to become fit, but until you break poor nutritional habits and learn to prepare new, healthier menus, you may need some competent guidance.

The Dean Ornish nutritional plan is a competent one and is readily available in his books and the hospitals and clinics that feature his popular regimen. Dr. Ornish's regimen is particularly useful because it does not require expensive diet foods or advocate strange eating practices. It combines good nutrition with appropriate exercise and mandatory support groups.

Some books on nutrition become best-sellers because of attractive marketing and catchy ideas, but they promote gimmicks or some clever "new" formula for nutrition. I encourage you to buy wisely or use your library card and the Internet selectively when exploring nutritional information. The nutritional books listed in the bibliography are not the only good ones, but they are sound.

Mental and Spiritual Practices. Certain mental-spiritual practices can also aid healthful eating and good digestion. Eating smarter includes relaxation, simplicity, savoring, and thankfulness. Relaxation aids digestion, as we know. But eating in an unhurried manner makes eating itself less compulsive, so thereby we can eat less, more comfortably. Savoring food is literally an art of nutrition. By becoming aware of aromas, enjoying the sight of simple, healthful food, eating more slowly, and tasting flavors more consciously we engage our senses and satisfy mental-spiritual needs as well as physical needs. But for many of us the pleasure of savoring our food may have to be adjusted from the acquired and addictive cravings for junk food and highly processed foods, to the appreciation of natural flavors in fresh and less-processed foods. Such savoring includes enjoying not only simple, basic foods but artistic food presentations and gourmet preparation and combinations. You will know you have accomplished something worthwhile when you reach this level of savoring.

Substituting prayer for unnecessary eating is a valuable behavior. For a discussion of this topic, see Shamblin's *The Weigh Down Diet*, listed in the bibliography.

Thankfulness is the spiritual nutrition component of a meal, in that you recognize the gracious source of this nutritional event. Even if saying grace at the beginning of a meal is standard practice, it should not be done perfunctorily. Taking time to be truly thankful for smaller portions of food is an enlightening and freeing experience. Eating with a thankful attitude and closing the meal with thankfulness and a commitment to stewardship and service help us stay conscious of the spiritual meaning of nutrition whether we eat alone or with others. I am not pushing piousness; I am encouraging openness to the spiritual dimensions of good nutrition in your quest for body-mind-spirit fitness.

Simple Rules about Food and Drink. What time of day we eat and when we eat in relation to strenuous work or exercise seem to make a difference in digestion and weight gain or loss, although some nutritionists say only the accumulated quantities of ingredients make a difference. Most of us learn the realities of our own body biochemistry through trial and error.

Of course, consult your pharmacist if you are unsure about interactions of medications with food or drink.

Take time to read ingredient lists and "nutritional facts" charts on the food products you buy. Though this adds a little time to grocery shopping, it will make you more aware of calories and of the relative values of protein, carbohydrates, fats, sodium, vitamins, and minerals. These food and ingredient guides remind us that no one else can make us healthy or keep us from ingesting unhealthy substances. We must learn to do this ourselves. And this is one of the primary messages of fitness.

"Functional foods," or "nutriceuticals" are a new category of foods in which artificial or healthier ingredients replace unhealthy ingredients in natural foods or add needed minerals and vitamins to foods that ordinarily do not contain much of such ingredients. Some fats are being replaced by manufactured compounds such as benecol in margarine. The future seems bright—and expensive—for such health enhancers, if government research and regulations keep up with marketing claims. Simplicity is ever a good guideline.

Which foods we eat makes an enormous difference, as we all know now. Competent nutritionists are helping us understand the effects of food combinations. Some gurus, however, seem to be playing on heightened fears through warnings and the sale of presumed remedies. Herbal fads abound in this essentially unregulated marketplace. Yet the growing awareness of natural, organically grown foods, along with wise use of herbs, can enhance healthful nutrition.

Be aware of food colorings, preservatives, fillers, and flavor enhancers in your food. Not only people with food allergies suffer from ingesting nonnutritional ingredients—all of us accumulate nocuous and toxic substances in our bodies from the food we eat. Nonnutritional ingredients force our bodies to use energy and biochemical resources to neutralize these unhealthful materials, or to store or eliminate them as safely as possible. Carcinogens are an example. Eating fresh or minimally processed foods and ensuring that the food is clean are important safeguards. My reading of the literature of nutrition over the past several years is that an additional warning is urgent—cut way down on "the three deadly white powders," as a some nutritionists call them: sugar, salt, and processed white flour.

Hydration is such an important part of nutrition that we cannot take it for granted. Remind yourself often that ordinary pure water is crucial to health and fitness. Our bodies are composed mostly of water. The process of hydration is continuous. It is crucial to oxidation, lubrication, cleansing, and purging. Our biochemical processes come to a halt if fluid levels are not adequate. Being "dehydrated" means the loss of more than one percent of our body's fluid, and this can happen rapidly, through exertion, injury, illness, low humidity in the air, or simply an inadequate intake of liquids. Our immune systems, mucous membranes, energy levels, and thought processes are particularly vulnerable to inadequate fluid intake.

Nutritionists generally recommend that a person drink eight glasses (8 ounces per glass) of fluid each day. Pure water is by far the best fluid to ingest in quantity, for it does not require the body to process all the other ingredients popular commercial beverages contain. We are fortunate to have potable water readily available in most parts of this country. The recent trend toward drinking more and more flavored sodas is worrisome because these typically contain sweeteners, sodium, caffeine, preservatives, artificial colorings, and alcohol, none of which is good for us in the amounts Americans typically ingest. And consumption of more healthful drinks like milk, fruit juices, and pure water declines as soda consumption increases. It is not hard to recognize the influence of advertising and social pressure in this trend.

While we are thinking of water as part of fitness, we can remind ourselves of the value of cleansing. Thoroughly washing our hands and our food is seen as increasingly more important as we understand more about various contaminants and how we can aid our immune system by eliminating many contaminants and pathogens by washing. Metaphorically, this is a reminder of the continuing need for cleansings of all kinds in body, mind, and spirit.

Fasting. Another important subject in healthful nutrition is fasting, but this is one of those terms that comes loaded with biases and misconceptions. One book in the bibliography focuses on fasting (Joel Fuhrman's *Fasting and Eating for Health*), and several others mention it positively. You probably know something about fasting, theologically as well as nutritionally, but you may not know how valuable it is for physical, mental, and spiritual health.

There are several forms of fasting: total fasting (only water is ingested), limited fasting (ingestion is limited to certain foods and beverages), variable fasting (ingestables vary during the fast), and brief fasting (missing one meal, eliminating one type of food or beverage, or not eating for a whole day). Fasting, as used here, means elimination of all food and beverages other than water, unless otherwise specified, for more than one day.

Most healthy and normally functioning persons could go without any food for many days without serious damage to health. Going without fluids is possible for only two to three days without damage. Anyone with medical problems or on medication should not fast without consulting a physician or professional nutritionist. To be on the safe side, in fact, no one should fast without first discussing it with a physician.

Fasting is becoming fashionable in spiritual formation again. The Bible speaks of it often. Jesus certainly did it. It has an honored place in church history and in some religious traditions even now. Fasting is valuable spiritually as a gift to God and a personal discipline. It is valuable mentally because it frees us from distractions. It is valuable physically for many reasons. But many of us will have to train ourselves into this discipline. We learn by doing it.

Fasting allows the body to rest from digestive efforts and begin to purge itself of stored toxins. These effects begin early in the fast and are obviously beneficial. Long-term effects are weight loss and healing of known and unknown maladies of the body. Dr. Joel Fuhrman, in *Fasting and Eating for Health*, discusses the copious medical and scientific data that indicates that fasting helps the body heal itself of many minor illnesses and diseases. Noting that it is typical, when we are ill or seriously injured, to not want to eat for a while, he argues that our bodies want to devote energy to the healing process under such conditions and have adequate stored nutritional resources to do this without food intake (water will still be necessary).

A one- or two-day fast is helpful but produces little long-term benefit. Its best use seems to be as an occasional or regular adjunct to a healthful nutritional regimen. Fasts of three or more days bring significant benefits, but require more planning and supportive conditions. Though many people and many studies cited indicate that most people can go about their lives almost normally while doing limited fasting, some people find serious fasting to be uncomfortable and enervating. After fasting several times I have learned, personally, that with successive fasts less effort is required, and the benefits become obvious.

My own experience with fasting helped me become aware of and understand bodily functions much better. I had fasted sporadically for Lent and other occasions in the past, but tried my first significant fast as experience for writing this book. My spouse and I did an eight-day fast, with plenty of pre-planning. The first day was a cutback day in which we ate only small portions of fruit and vegetables. The second day began five days of total fasting, drinking only water. The last two days were reentry days in which we ate small portions of fruit on day seven, and larger portions of fruits and leafy vegetables on the eighth day. For several days after the fast we ate only fruits and vegetables, before returning to our usual eating practices.

During this fast we noticed a decrease in energy and experienced some sporadic physical discomfort, along with expected changes in elimination. But all of this was manageable, even exhilarating occasionally. We found it very helpful to do this together instead of alone. And we would advise doing it only when work conditions and social obligations are compatible.

As for the benefits, we both lost a significant amount of weight, and we saved a week's grocery bills. We learned much about our bodies and about corollary mental and spiritual effects. When we resumed eating, even the limited reentry eating provided near-euphoric enjoyment and savoring of food. And after the fast we found it much easier to adjust our eating habits to a more healthful mode, which we now continue. We tend to feel more energy, consistently, now. The weight loss lowered blood pressure for each of us significantly. And at my annual physical exam last month, all my vital signs and lab tests showed significant improvement. We expect to do limited and total fasts occasionally for the rest of our lives. It is now a valued part of our fitness regimens.

It is beyond the purview of this book to provide specific diets, menus, and weight-loss regimens. I have found reliable information about these things in the books listed in the bibliography. I hope you will find information that works for you, if you haven't already. Pay attention to the credentials and experience of those who provide nutritional information. This is a "hot" field now, in terms of public interest and commercial benefits. Vitamin-mineral-herbal supplements alone are a $12 billion per year business in the United States. All kinds of professionals, gurus, and "experts" are making claims and selling things we may or may not need. This is why I ask you repeatedly in this book to *think* with me and evaluate things for yourself—even what I say. There are few experts in nutrition. But a growing number of professionals are trying to help us understand bodily nutrition—and even more are trying to sell us products and systems that may not be helpful. Buyer beware. Jonathan Swift, the esteemed English satirist, is purported to have said, "The best doctors in the world are Dr. Diet, Dr. Quiet, and Dr. Merryman."

"C" STANDS FOR CONGRUENCY

WHAT ARE THE BASIC RELATIONSHIPS OF FITNESS?

Several systems are involved in nutritional fitness, and they are related and interactive. One such system is our own personhood, our unique body, mind, and spirit. Since I have been noting this relatedness continually, the only reminder necessary here is that, just as we must think carefully about what we ingest and how it relates to physical needs and functioning, we must apply these insights to how we nurture our minds and spirits. Mental and spiritual junk foods are as nocuous as the junk food we buy in foodstores. The disciplinary task for many of us is to break the pleasure bond that ties us to the wrong kinds of food in our society. We can then develop a bond between good nourishment and the satisfactions that accrue in fitness. Good food tastes as good as bad food, when we retrain our appetites.

Another system is the ecological system. The growth, processing, and marketing of healthful food benefits the ecological system because this is what the ecology produces most naturally. However, with the population explosion comes the need to grow and process ever more food. This means the use of more pesticides, more herbicides, more growth hormones, more inappropriate water use, and most of all, more investment of time and capital by businesses interested in selling more and more of what they decide to produce instead of what is realistically needed. Fitness must include the whole of our ecology, for it is an interactive, interdependent system.

Family, spouse, colleagues, close friends, parishioners . . . many will experience some effects from your fitness quest. We can simplify this issue by remembering that personal fitness choices, if they are health-ful, will usually have beneficial effects on those close to us.

Before leaving this nutrition section, review by asking yourself, What ABCs have I learned about nutrition for bodily fitness?

A–Awareness: Simplicity, attitude, body-mind-spirit fitness are potent motivations.

B–Basics: Eat smart; eat less; eat nutritious food,; hydrate.

C–Congruency: Nutrition is an interrelationship of nourishing resources.

EXERCISE

We turn now to the exercise component of bodily fitness. A quotation from James B. Nelson's book *Embodiment* can focus our attention: "The way we think and feel about ourselves as bodies will always find expression in the way we think and feel about the world and about God."

Sometimes I look at my body and ask how it can be a temple of God. At other times I look and think it is a very special body chapel. We have a rational and scientific explanation for how our human bodies came into existence. Yet there cannot be a full explanation without account-ing for the spiritual dimension. And there will always be mystery. Are we bodily beings having a spiritual experience, or spiritual beings hav-ing a bodily experience . . . or both?

The apostle Paul was obsessed with the human body, no doubt as a by-product of the philosophical dualism of his day. This later produced a theological dualism regarding body and spirit that yet influences Western thinking. Paul suffered agonies of guilt about his body (Rom. 7:14–25) that were assuaged by his euphoric concept of salvation as freedom from the condemnation he felt when enslaved to his "flesh" (Rom. 8:1–17). So powerful was his concept of the body that he built his idea of salvation around the embodiment of Christ in flesh, which could then become the bloody sacrifice of redemption. The resurrec-tion of a bodily Christ provided the concept of the community of faith as the continuing embodiment of Jesus Christ on earth (1 Cor. 3:16–17). Personally, he not only struggled with guilt about his body, but he seems to have experienced physical disability of some sort ("thorn in the flesh," 2 Cor. 12:7), which kept the body in his attention, as a reminder of the need for humility.

Our physical bodies are a powerful metaphor for the full experience of living, mentally and spiritually. We recognize sometime in our early years that each of us is sui generis, with some tendencies toward self-centeredness, anxieties about being normal, and fears of being ignored. We're all the same . . . in different ways.

Intense, even masochistic exercise can be a troubled reaction to dislike for the body, or a guilty response to self-abuse of the bodies. Other psychic wounds or obsessive-compulsive tendencies can induce counter-productive fervor in exercising and stressing the body. Healthy self-management notes and heals such excessive tendencies and treats the body with respect and thoughtfulness as body-mind-spirit fitness is sought.

In 1999, the President's Council on Fitness, updating its Healthy People 2000 project, reported that Americans have missed the goal of having 30 percent of us doing at least thirty minutes of moderate activity five days of the week. This despite all the media warnings telling of the correlation between physical activity and body weight and health. Apparently we are not yet frightened enough or tired enough of paying the enormous bills associated with unfitness to change.

Memos concerning Exercise

The following sections discuss general issues that inform physical exercise and physical fitness regimens.

Movement. Physical movement is not as simple as it seems. It requires energy, space, time, decisions. Developing physical exercise into a regular regimen may involve kinetics, ergonomics, entropy, and synergy, and all are worth exploring. But your primary concern here is to get comfortable with structured movements designed to flex, tone, and strengthen muscle clusters and the whole body. A good beginning is to simply stand, sit, lie down in a space big enough for free movement, and then just move your body or parts of it spontaneously and randomly. Let yourself explore various movements and note physical sensations and what your body does easily. Note what movements feel comfortable and which ones do not.

Next, try some familiar movements and exercises. Note how to position your body so that these movements are more comfortable and graceful. For position is important as a beginning for exercise. Doing an exercise with a distorted body position can be dangerous.

Note what happens when you repeat a familiar exercise several times (repetitions, or "reps"). What happens when you slow the repetitions or speed them up? What happens when you do them intensely versus more casually? What happens to your body configuration and to primary muscles as you stimulate them with many reps? What happens to your breathing? Do you know how to manage energy expenditure so that you do not exhaust yourself quickly (pacing)?

Posture-Therapeutic Movement. We know that good posture is visually attractive, and in recent years posture has been emphasized as therapeutic and important to health. Correct alignment of head, shoulders, and legs with a normally curved and vertically aligned spine induces and allows good physical, mental, and spiritual functioning. Many of us have learned the value of standing and sitting straight, both for its bodily effects and for the confidence and sense of well-being that accompany good posture. Good posture is a companion to positive attitudes.

Over time, there have been several schools of posture-movement therapy and exercise. Late in the nineteenth century Frederick Matthias Alexander, an Australian actor, learned the value of good posture for performance and health and began to teach his posture therapy. In 1892 Andrew Taylor Still, an American army physician, established the American School of Osteopathy in order to teach his methods of stimulating the body's self-healing powers. Still taught that disturbances in the musculoskeletal system affect other body parts, causing disorders correctable by manipulation techniques along with conventional medicine. Also in the 1890s Daniel D. Palmer developed a basic theory of spine-brain-body connection, and then a spine manipulation method that has been popularized in several forms as chiropractic medical practice. It emphasizes release of stress on nerves emanating from the spine in order to alleviate pain and promote healthy functioning of nerves that control muscles and organs. Moshe Feldenkrais, Joseph Heller, Ida Rolf, Milton Trager, Alexander Lowen, and more recently Jean Houston and others have pioneered therapies based on posture, skeletal alignment, and therapeutic movement and manipulation. Yoga, massage and healing touch therapies, acupuncture, acupressure, and disciplined self-movement regimens such as bioenergetics and t'ai chi offer unique self-managed or practitioner-induced body treatments that many people have found beneficial. Even traditional medical practitioners now recognize the values of some "alternative" or "complementary" therapies.

The concept and practice of balance is also important to the body-mind-spirit therapies and lifestyles. This includes physical balance in posture and exercise and balance as a self-management discipline. Balance means equilibrium, symmetry, and proportion in the development of harmony between body parts, mind, spirit, and the way we manage them. A physical, mental, and spiritual sense of balance in our lives is important to relaxation, confidence, and serenity. Our bodies, minds, and spirits seek homeostasis, but we often interfere with this through poor health practices, distressed lifestyles, addictions, and ignoring body-mind-spirit connections. Part of body-mind-spirit fitness is sensitivity to natural homeostasis.

Breathing. Of course you know that breathing is important in physical activity and exercise. But what do you know about regulating your breathing, how breathing works, when to breathe in a particular exercise, how to deepen your breathing, the relationship of breathing to endurance, and so on? Pay attention to breathing as the life-sustaining and energizing dynamic that is central to all you do. And note that deep breathing has much to do with fitness.

Much of the recent research and writing on health and fitness includes an emphasis on proper (deep, slow, concentrated) breathing. Notable proponents include Herbert Benson ("Relaxation Response") and Jon Kabat-Zinn ("Mindfulness," which includes learning to breath in healing, healthful ways). Be sure to build a consciousness of breathing in your body-mind-spirit fitness.

Imaging. Exercise and physical activity work best when you have a mental image of the exercise and of yourself doing it. We know that our minds guide physical activity, but this guidance is more than a brain sending signals to muscles to do a particular action. When our minds think of the action beforehand, we are preparing our whole person to participate. We are also setting a mood and attitude. And we are answering the question of why we are doing this.

Our minds participate during the activity too, of course. Again this is more than a brain sending signals to muscles. For our minds process how we want to do the exercise, how intensely, and how long. All of this feeds back to and from the original mental image and decision to do this action.

Then there is the aftermath in which the action and its consequences are reviewed and evaluated. Much of this is subconscious, yet since it is important to self-management and growth in fitness, you can aid your development by making this whole process conscious. After you settle into a regimen of fitness activities, you will not need to be so conscious of this process. But at the beginning, or when changing patterns, it is important to develop this rationality.

Timing. *When* you exercise is important to your success. If you exercise at the beginning of the day, the effects are somewhat different from those of exercise at midday or later in the day. No one time is best for all, for each of us has comfort levels and times when exercise feels most compatible with the rest of the day. And for many of us, our daily and weekly work schedules determine when fitness routines must be done.

Biorhythms are the silent partners to any physical activity. Biorhythms are the ebb and flow of our biochemistry, in which our moods, energy levels, and mental acuity are influenced strongly by the interaction of hormones, enzymes, peptides, neurotransmitters, and so on.

Several hundred biochemical cycles and rhythms have been identified in the human body. They occur as lifelong cycles ranging from the twenty-four-hour circadian rhythm of alternating cycles to the split-second molecular interaction among our cells and organs. Nearly all of them function without our conscious attention, except for the consequences when these rhythms are balanced or not. Yet they are the dynamics of our life-sustaining biochemistry—they are built in, and this ties them into any plan for body-mind-spirit fitness. The more fit we are, the more likely it is that these biochemical interactions will be efficient and effective in sustaining health and growth.

This field of biochemistry is called chronobiology, or more recently, chronobiometry. Physicians, biologists, chemists, nutritionists, pharmacologists, and other scientists have been researching human biochemistry for years, of course. But more recently their data has indicated that nearly all human activity is heavily influenced by our biochemical cycles and rhythms. We typically are conscious of only our feelings and ability to accomplish tasks, but if we raise our awareness to what is going on inside our bodies and minds, we can manage ourselves more healthfully. Many good intentions and sincere efforts toward fitness are sabotaged by biochemistry, so it is important to become more aware of your body and mind in your fitness quest. More positively, there is a joy and thankfulness dimension in our growing fitness that comes as we realize by experience and feelings that we are "fearfully and wonderfully made" (Ps. 139:14). Moreover, by becoming sensitive to personal rhythms and cycles, you then can become aware of biochemical effects occurring in families, congregations, and in the whole geofamily and earthly ecology. Since we believe God created these powerful, interactive forces, they help us understand God's purposes.

Timing, as related to fitness, also includes regularity. Though it can contribute to boredom, doing a fitness activity, particularly exercise, at the same time each day and week consistently will help it become a habit. You can vary your routines, but you should stay with a workable schedule. Habitual practice reduces the energy and time you will spend on schedule conflicts, mental resistance, and distractions. You simply do the fitness activities because now is the time this is done, and because you know it is worthwhile.

Pain. Feelings of pain and comfort are highly effective teachers. They are especially significant for fitness, for they are indicators of mistakes and progress in a fitness quest. However, pain and comfort are not reliable guidelines for physical activities without appropriate interpretation. For example, someone in a deconditioned state (out of shape) will find it somewhat painful to return to good physical condition. And it feels so comfortable and comforting sometimes to stop strenuous exercise that we are tempted to abort fitness activities. On the other hand, discomfort tells us when we are pushing beyond our usual physical thresholds. Pain (stronger than discomfort) is a serious indicator, for pain tells us that we are in danger of injury, or that we have been injured and are not yet healed, or that we are sick or doing the exercise incorrectly. It is not true that we must experience sustained pain in order to achieve fitness ("No pain—no gain" is wrong). Yet we must push ourselves beyond present comfort levels as our fitness progresses, to a new and more healthful comfort level. But this is largely a semantic problem: we misuse the words "discomfort" and "pain."

Intensity level, duration, and type of pain are significant. If pain is excruciating, you must seek relief, which often means stopping intense exertion. If pain persists, you must check for deeper causes. If pain is sharp, it likely indicates injury; if throbbing, it likely indicates strain or structural disorder; if the pain is an ache, it likely indicates overexertion or illness. All these are idiosyncratic, of course. But if pain is intense or chronic, consult a professional.

Comfort is so desirable that some social observers say physical, mental, and spiritual comforts are the primary motivators of human experience. Comfort in itself, however, is an unreliable priority. For it can become addictive in various forms. It can trigger resistance, excuses, and avoidance of the exertions and changes necessary in a fitness quest.

Pain and comfort are mental and spiritual phenomena as well as being physical experiences. I note this only briefly here as a reminder of the body-mind-spirit connection but will return to this idea in later chapters.

Nutrition. This subject was discussed earlier, but a note on the significance of nutrition in relationship to exercise is appropriate here. First of all, good nutrition and appropriate exercise are necessary partners in body-mind-spirit fitness. Second, good nutrition generates more energy for physical activities. Third, good nutrition and appropriate exercise facilitate each other and add to the benefits of each. Neither is an adequate substitute for the other, however.

EXERCISE AND THE ABCS

The ABCs motif will serve again as a way to organize your thinking and move toward a transformation of your present bodily state into "being the best that you can be" . . . your fitness quest.

"A" STANDS FOR AWARENESS

WHAT DO I KNOW OR NEED TO KNOW ABOUT PHYSICAL EXERCISE AND FITNESS?

"Eating less—eating sensibly is only one-half of the fitness balancing act. Physical activity is the other—very important—half of the equation. Remember: if you eat more calories than you burn, you'll gain weight. In other words, you pay the price in pounds if you don't 'move!' So exercise really is the dieter's best friend" (From *On Your Way to Fitness,* by C. Everett Koop, p. 3).

Most of us know that appropriate exercise is beneficial and very important for fitness. We know that regular exercise and an active lifestyle induce the body to produce more HDL, the beneficial kind of cholesterol that helps cleanse arteries of the fatty plaque deposits that clog blood vessels. And we know that active people produce much less insulin and that decreases the likelihood of adult-onset diabetes. We also know, however, that knowledge does not equal practice. Therefore we must actually exercise in beneficial ways in order to achieve fitness. This is a particularly complicated issue for people with physical disabilities, people recovering from serious illness or injury, or for those who are seriously out of shape physically. Many of us have individual limitations and variations, but a full discussion of all these variations is not in the purview of this discussion. Therefore, each reader must adapt the exercises and regimens offered here to her or his personal conditions. For specific guidance related to disabilities, medical conditions, and obesity, be sure to consult appropriate specialists.

Let's assume that you are beginning structured exercise for the first time. You will need to teach yourself how to experience your body and its reactions as you do each exercise. Take some time to explore your physical self (a full-length mirror is helpful). Touch each part of your body and take time to think how it is constructed and how it works. As you touch, squeeze, press, rub each of your body parts, notice not only how each feels to your hand, but how each part responds to your touch. Explore your muscles and bone joints particularly, for the striated muscles and ligaments are our focus here. They have individual and coordinated functions.

How a muscle or set of muscles feels in response to physical activity is an indicator of its condition (flexibility and strength). In a relaxed state muscles produce little conscious feeling. In exercise they can produce feelings of strength, tiredness, or pain, which are significant indicators about exercise routines and regimens. As used here, the words "routine" or "pattern" refer to specific exercises and activities, while the word "regimen" refers to a regular series of exercises and activities.

"B" STANDS FOR BASICS

WHAT ARE BASIC RESOURCES AND EXPERIENCES FOR PHYSICAL EXERCISE IN FITNESS?

In what follows I provide information, suggested equipment, and exercise-activity regimens that fit the modest but disciplined approach to fitness offered in this book. Much more information is available in the books listed in the bibliography, and I recommend you consult them. Consider going on to a higher level of fitness if this feels appropriate.

Types of Exercise. It is beyond the purview of this book to discuss and evaluate all kinds of exercise and physical activity important to fitness. And we should remind ourselves often that there is no one best exercise or regimen for all persons. Neither are all exercises appropriate or necessary for personal fitness. Following are some categories of exercises that review the possibilities for developing or revising a physical fitness regimen:

Muscle-flexing, toning, aerobic, and strengthening exercises include warm-ups such as stretching, bending, slow twisting, rolling; isometrics (tensing a muscle without flexing it); isotonics (flexing muscles against resistance repeatedly); aerobics (continuous exercise designed to improve oxygen utilization and endurance); cross-training (mixing types of exercises); and strength training (done with any type weights/reps, machines). These can be done alone or with partners.

Games include athletic competition (baseball, soccer, volleyball, tennis, racquetball, etc.) and recreation (individual or partner activities without intense competition, such as fishing, golfing, dancing, hiking, skiing).

Nonexercises is a category of lesser known but valuable activities. These include body postures and movements that focus on natural shapes and motions, such as flexing, extension, and coordination rather than strength or aerobics. An example is study and development of gentle bodily movement, kinesiology. Names such as Alexander, Feldenkrais, Mezieres, and Houston are associated with such programs.

Stress reducers are relatively unorganized activities designed to stretch and relax tense muscles. Included are stretches, massage, manipulation of muscles and bone structures, as well as relaxation techniques such as Herbert Benson's "relaxation response," Jon Kabat-Zinn's "mindfulness," yoga, biofeedback, and others. Explore which ones, and which combinations, are effective for you. You may already have some routines you use as quick, frequent resources in breaking stress buildups as you go through the day. Beginning the day in a relaxed mode, of course, is crucial, for not only does this set a pattern, it provides a memory for the day to remind yourself of how valuable it is to reduce body-mind-spirit tension. I like to take several breaks during the day in which I concentrate on stretching my arms, flexing my neck and shoulders, and rotating my upper torso, with my eyes closed, and then sitting quietly for a moment to regain a mental picture of relaxation and peace. Often I include my legs and feet in brief stretching-flexing movements. A prayer of thankfulness and union-communion with God completes the respite.

Stretching-flexing. Standing, sitting, or lying down, slowly stretch your arms as far as you can reach (up and out) and hold each position for a few counts. Next, slowly rotate your head from side to side, and backward and forward, as far as possible. Now stand with feet apart at shoulder width, hands on hips, and rotate your torso as far as possible in both directions (several reps). Vary this by doing the same motions while bent at the waist. Then windmill your extended arms to touch each foot with each hand alternately. Some deep knee bends (without bouncing) will stretch and relax your legs. Rise up on tiptoes for a few counts and down. If you can slowly bend backward over a hassock or stool (cover it with a pillow for comfort), letting your head hang backward and down as far as possible, hold this position for a few counts. Hanging by your arms from a sturdy bar anchored to both sides of a doorway will have a traction effect and release tension in your shoulders. If you have appropriate equipment, hanging upside down also

adds a traction effect that decompresses the spine. Tensing and relaxing each fist, especially if you hold the tension tightly for a several
counts, can bring a pleasant sense of relaxation in the arms and hands.
Sitting with one leg at a time stretched out, and rotating and stretching each foot several times, relaxes calf, ankle, and foot. Lean the small
of your back against the edge of your desk or table, with your hands
holding the desk edge, then lean backward several times. Cat stretches
relieve tension as you get on all fours and arch your back upward and
downward. You may want to extend this stretching by putting your
head down on your hands with your hips remaining straight up over
your knees. (Illustrations of these stretching-flexing exercises can be
found in Appendix A.)

Posture aids. Dale Anderson, M.D., suggests that when you're sitting (at a desk, driving, in meetings, or even in a hospital waiting room)
periodically place one fist in the small of your back to encourage proper
curvature. Develop a sitting posture of keeping your head as high as
possible and directly above your hips. Periodically tilt your head back
as far as possible, then sit as if an offering plate is balanced on your
head, relaxing more each time.

Physical prayer combines the physical, mental, and spiritual aspects
of physical activity. This is one of my favorite categories. I have culled and
learned these simple activities over many years and am indebted to several disciplines for offering them. From silent retreats, both Ignatian and
Benedictine, I learned to walk, kneel, and sit in contemplation and serenity. From yoga and transcendental meditation I learned relaxation posture and deep breathing. From t'ai chi, judo, and military training I
learned to discipline my body for intense physical action. From football,
basketball, softball, and handball I learned to push my body to its limits
to achieve a goal. From loving intimacy, parenting, pastoring, and pastoral counseling I learned to pay attention to physical behavior, disabilities, and the body-mind-spirit connection. From extraordinary physical
therapists, nurses, physicians, chiropractors, and masseuses and masseurs
I learned the value of relaxing, caring, healing touch. From psychosynthesis (Roberto Assagioli), Alexander training, and Jean Houston I
learned the power of physical movement when tuned to spiritual rhythms.
And from my colleagues and clients in spiritual retreats I learned the awesome spiritual interactions that come from sharing the sacraments, foot
washing, foot massage, religious dance, weeping and intercession
together, and charismatic combinations of movement and music. From
innumerable poets, philosophers, graphic artists, and musicians I learned
the nurture that occurs when an open spirit, a healthy mind, and a will-

ing body participate in artistic movement in spirit-mind-body. From my father and my own experience I have learned the simplicity and value of walking (briskly or slowly) combined with meditation. And from God I am learning the joy and responsibility of creative stewardship of body-mind-spirit through the agency of the *imago Dei*. Physical prayer is part of my daily exercise regimen, I encourage you to consider including it in your physical activities.

Daily Regimen. I have studied so many good daily fitness routines (regimens) that it is hard to recommend just one or even two. The books listed in the bibliography offer several that I find to be sensible and useful in a variety of situations. Instead of promoting one of these, however, I simply suggest that each person try some simple combinations of stretching, flexing, and exercising each body area (neck, shoulders, arms, back, hips, legs, and feet) until a compatible routine is developed that leaves you feeling limber, loose, and invigorated. Since I am a morning person, I prefer doing these early, and perhaps repeating some of them at various times of the day, especially on days when I do a lot of sitting.

My daily exercise regimen includes at least one aerobic activity in addition to the early morning exercise combinations suggested above. "Power walks" are now my aerobic activity of choice. Knee problems preclude jogging, handball, volleyball, and the other joint-impact activities I used to enjoy. But walking is satisfactory, as long as it includes a vigorous pace and as much upper body movement as possible. Swimming is often recommended, and jogging is a favorite aerobic activity, but I highly recommend walking because it is readily available, requires no exotic equipment, can be done on your own schedule, and is inexpensive. Walk as vigorously as possible, for at least half an hour, five days per week.

I have a bias for simplicity in my exercising, so that I can maintain my regimen when traveling as well as at home. I have tried and given away exercise equipment until I now have only a small trampoline (for light jogging in place, and when weather precludes walking outdoors), and some small free weights for toning upper body and legs. A good pair of cross-training shoes and loose-fitting clothing completes my equipment needs. Changing the setting, combinations, and schedule for these activities helps prevent boredom. You may find other possibilities that work well for you.

It is important that you warm up and cool down if you are doing strenuous exercises. Warm-ups are stretching, flexing, and gentle aerobics that get muscles ready for more intense activities. Cool-downs include gentle, relaxing movements, or fewer and slower reps of the vigorous exercises you were doing so the body slows its pace while maintaining good circulation and breathing.

"C" Stands for Congruency

How do my awareness and resources for fitness combine and fit with my relationships and responsibilities?

Sometimes all these issues and activities fit together readily. Sometimes we must simply combine them as best we can. It is a mistake to expect that fitness, even at its highest level, will make life idyllic. But it is true that body-mind-spirit fitness feels better and makes it more likely that we will handle life and ministry more effectively and be open to change and growth.

Think of how physical exercise and fitness function in your life. Are these things a regular part of your life? If not, what negative consequences are you living with that could be improved through a fitness quest? If body-mind-spirit fitness is now part of your life, what growth do you plan? And how are you sharing the benefits of BMS fitness with others?

As I review the physical fitness part of my life, I find it is consistent with my understanding of union-communion with God and ecology. It is congruent with my image of myself. It is congruent with my call to be an ordained pastor and pastoral counselor. It is shared with my spouse, family, and close friends, so it is congruent with my primary intimate relationships. And it is congruent with my desire to be open to growth and change through God's purposes.

The emphasis on discipline and self-management in this chapter does not imply that self-centeredness is the key to fitness. Rather, this emphasis is intended to counter the lack of disciplined self-management that is common among clergy. It is God's grace that makes all this work together for what is good for us, for our intimates and constituents, and for God's purposes. God's grace, however, is operative most effectively in spiritually disciplined believers.

SUMMARY

In this chapter in a series of memos I noted the body-mind-spirit connections, distinguished between bodily image and actual body, checked

on motivation for fitness, defined and discussed energy, reviewed stewardship, and noted informational resources. I discussed nutrition in its
various forms, including the latest guidelines, along with fasting. I
explored the many aspects of bodily exercise and nonexercise, including physical prayer and stress reducers, and emphasized discipline in its
positive forms. And I described a daily regimen for exercise. In chapter
6 I will give similar treatment to mental fitness.

6

Mental Fitness

> Finally, beloved, whatever is true, whatever is
> honorable, whatever is just, whatever is pure,
> whatever is pleasing, whatever is commendable, if there
> is any excellence and if there is anything worthy of praise,
> think about these things.
> *Philippians 4:8*

The mental part of fitness is more complicated than the physical part because we know less about our brains and hearts and less about how to nurture and manage them, and because the consequences of how we manage them are less obvious. Further, we don't even know what we don't know about the brain-heart-body connections.

But we are learning. And part of what we are learning is that we have more control over what goes on in our brain-heart-mind than we realize. This is good news for your fitness quest. For as you become more aware of what mental fitness is and find some guidelines for achieving it, you are likely to improve not only mental functioning but also the body-mind connection.

The terminology I use here may include information and concepts new to many. Therefore some clarification is important. From here on, I use the terms "mind" and "mental" to include the functions of both the brain and heart, as well as the cognitive (thought) and affective (emotions) categories of cognition and consciousness. This term also includes implications that other organs of our bodies also "think" in some fashion.

The brain and heart are physical organs, of course. But their functions include far more than regulation of the body's biochemistry. The latest brain and heart research indicates that thinking and knowing are more complicated than we had thought. And the cognition within human beings is part of a universal thinking-knowing process that is occurring and interacting in all living things. This is systems theory writ large. You are probably aware of enormous strides in brain research but may not be as acquainted with the dramatic research on the thinking of the heart and other organs. Space and intent are inadequate in this book for full explanations of such important research and theorizing. Those interested in more information will find it in *The Heart's Code*, by Paul Pearsall; *The HeartMath Solution*, by Doc Childre and Howard Martin; *The Soul's Code*, by James Hillman; and *The Humanizing Brain*, by James Ashbrook and Carol Albright, all listed in the bibliography.

As I noted earlier, mental capacities as well as physical capacities vary in individuals. Therefore the goal of body-mind-spirit fitness is not for all to be the same or for some to be better than others. Rather, the goal is that all of us become the best that we can be, each with our idiosyncrasies, and that we learn to support each other's personhood in order to enjoy the shared benefits of human synergy. Learning about human mental process contributes to both personhood and synergy.

The ABCs schema will organize understanding of mental fitness and the development of a mental fitness regimen. But first, take a look at the relevant memos of information and experience below.

MEMOS CONCERNING THE MIND

The Connection. Not only are body, mind, and spirit connected, but the mind is the most powerful and controlling partner in this relationship. For the mind receives, processes, interprets, and makes decisions about both body and spirit, as well as about its own functioning.

In fact, an issue of particular concern in the interconnections among body, mind, and spirit is this pervasive interpreting-controlling factor of the mind, which is automatic and done without much conscious awareness of it on our part. Recent research on the brain appears to indicate that memory, for example, is not the camera-perfect, factual process we had believed it to be. According to these findings our brain-mind receives data from our senses, then immediately refers it to areas of the brain that interpret it, and then stores these interpretations as memories. We then recall these memories of events, information, and experiences as factual and tend to believe our remembered version as factual truth, even when evidence shows otherwise.

The mind's interpreting-controlling factor is particularly important in regard to spiritual experience. For though many believe God can intervene directly in our lives on occasion, most of what we call revelation and spiritual insight comes to us through our senses and is therefore immediately filtered through this interpretation-control process. This is why spiritual "discernment" is so important. For we believe that one of the spiritual gifts is discernment, by which we can better distinguish between our personal and group interpretations on the one hand, and the realities of our world and God's truth on the other. We need to remind ourselves often that discernment is not simply an endorsement of what we want to believe. Rather, it is our best connection to God's "higher thoughts" and "higher ways" (Isa. 55:9) And it is always a gift from God attained only by grace and spiritual disciplines. (This will be discussed further in chapter 7, on spiritual fitness.)

The mind connections are also important for an increasingly recognized health issue, namely, the influence each organ can have on the others for sickness or healing. Though it is something of an oversimplification, we can say that sick thoughts tend to produce sick bodies, and a healthy mind tends to engender health in the body. This does not imply that genetic flaws or disabilities make us guilty of our illnesses and unfitness. But we can say that certain kinds of unhealthy thought patterns tend to induce sickness in certain organs or make the body vulnerable to specific diseases. And considerable scientific data support the opinion that specific kinds of healthy cerebration ("directed imaging") tend to induce health in specific parts of the body. The reverse also seems possible, although there is less data and support for this. The bibliography includes books that cover this issue more fully; see especially chapter 3 in Howard Clinebell's *Well Being*.

Consciousness. The literature on awareness, perception, and our conscious-unconscious selves is enormous. For our purposes here I use the generic term "awareness" to include all elements of consciousness. When we examine mental fitness, we need to note that besides the automatic consciousness we have developed over our lifetime, sensory data, intuition, and internal experience contributes to the expansion of these mental capacities.

A complicating factor in any discussion is the close connection between consciousness and unconsciousness. Consciousness means more than being awake; it also means insight, being aware of our personal thought processes. This is crucial to mental fitness. Beyond this is a vast, dynamic repository of memory, intuition, imagination, and habitual reference points, usually called the unconscious. Sometimes we distinguish between a "preconscious" part of the unconscious, which means that part which is closer to the surface—closer to conscious—and the rest of unconsciousness.

This unconscious part of ourselves has been compared to the underwater part of an iceberg: We can't see it, yet it is the foundation of consciousness—the part we can "see," or can be aware of. As with the iceberg, the unconscious part of our mind is hidden from our consciousness even while it supports and controls the conscious part of our mind in important ways. And, as the hidden part of the iceberg is influenced by such factors as water currents, cold, darkness, and the water itself, so the unconscious mind is influenced by unseen forces such as forgotten memories, intuition, spiritual beings, and archetypes (Carl Jung's name for the collective unconscious, or society's accumulated memory). The visible part of an iceberg is open to the influences of air currents, temperature changes, and sunlight, much as the conscious mind is influenced by visible, sensate, social factors. Both parts of the mind influence each other in predictable and unpredictable ways. We become aware of the presence and influences of the underwater part of an iceberg by observing its effects and interactions. And this is how we become aware of the influences of our unconscious minds. We recognize influences on our thinking and behavior that are not directly traceable to our conscious thoughts. The patterns of such influences give us clues concerning our unconscious self (mind). For example, when we notice that we are consistently afraid of water, we can search through experience to find causes. Or when we enjoy certain kinds of people, or foods, or worship experiences, we may be able to find reasons deep within ourselves and our history.

A pastoral application: Many of us can recall being fascinated when we first noticed how subconscious cues influenced relationships, church meetings and worship, and even our own feelings. How the chairs are arranged for a committee meeting, who speaks first, the temperature of the room, what clothing each person wears, and such, do have effects on meetings and relationships. When we ignore such subconscious cues we lose valuable pastoring insights.

Mental fitness is more than training the conscious mind to function in healthy ways. It includes becoming aware of the patterns and influences of the unconscious mind and working to transform these patterns if they are unhealthy. It includes being careful to build the kind of memories, habits, and influences in our lives that will accumulate as a healthy unconscious. The assistance provided by a certified pastoral counselor, a spiritual director, or a secularly trained mental health professional who values religious faith can help us understand and manage both our conscious and our unconscious minds.

Stimulation. The human organism lives by stimulation, or stress, as we usually name it. In fact, without it the body, the mind, and the spirit atrophy. Too much stimulation produces distress. Too little induces boredom. The right amount (balance) keeps our minds (and bodies and spirits) functioning as intended. Hans Selye used the terms "stress" (neutral), "distress" (negative), and "eustress" (positive) to categorize levels of stimulation and their effects.

Stimulation comes in many forms, and it affects body, mind and spirit together. We can, however, concentrate on stimuli that have the most direct effect on any of the three. For instance, we can stress the body through exercise, and thereby produce positive stimulation for the mind and spirit. We can be mentally creative and produce eustress for body and spirit. And we can have a valued worship experience that generates eustress for mind and body.

The intense interactions of persons, the generated cues of media and environment, and the voluntary or imposed obligations of work, play, and intimacy often produce more stimulation than is healthy for our bodies, minds, and spirits. Such distress must be managed in ways that guide us toward healthy functioning, without excessive and persistent strain. For we can grow in ability to manage all the stresses we encounter . . . up to a threshold determined by our physical, mental, and spiritual capacities. We can even exceed such thresholds occasionally, if we then allow for recovery from such supererogation.

It is now so common to exceed the limits of our capacity to handle stress in a healthful way that we have a popular name for it: burnout. We also have a popular name for the lack of desired stimulation: boredom. The commonness of these terms may mask the serious consequences they produce. We can use the term burnout to indicate persistent tiredness or intense dislike of working conditions and lifestyles, or as a plea for sympathy. We can even use it to indicate boredom, as when we engage in hard work or play that no longer produces adequate satisfaction. Boredom as a condition in itself may indicate lack of needed stimulation. Or it may indicate an obsessive desire for stimulation at unhealthy levels.

Both burnout and boredom are indicators of unfitness. They are wake-up calls. We should take them seriously, for they are not just unpleasant experience, they are signals from body, mind, and spirit that unfitness has deteriorated to the point of significant damage. There are early warning signals, and levels of burnout or boredom should be noted and evaluated if present. Continual anxiety, chronic mild depression, random floundering behavior, escapism, and such suggest that it is time for a checkup.

Biochemistry. The chemical interactions that occur in the mind are incredibly complicated, even for those who specialize in the study, healing, and training of the human mind. Much of the mind-brain's functioning is biochemical. Hormones, enzymes, peptides, and fluids interact in ways we can barely understand. But we do tend to notice and then recognize the consequences of how we nurture, use, and develop our biochemical selves. In chapter 5 I identified nutrition, hydration, and exercise as critical factors in physical functioning. Now I add mental needs and characteristics that are in large measure biochemical. The connection here is in recognizing that what we put in our mouths has significant biochemical consequences. So does what we put in our minds. Further, the way we nurture our bodies affects the biochemistry of our minds. Later we will note that how we nurture our bodies and our minds affects our spiritual biochemistry as well.

The organic brain part of our mind needs to maintain adequate fluid levels (hydration). It needs protein for replacing, rebuilding, and repairing cells and conduits. And it needs carbohydrates and fats in order to produce the glucose that is its fuel (energy). Vitamins and minerals in normal amounts complete the nutrition resources for the organic brain, along with the oxygenation provided by normal breathing. Learning to balance these is a key to mental fitness (review the bodily nutrition material in chapter 5).

The mind's biochemistry is not limited to the food we eat. Brain researchers, nutritionists, and people who have learned by experience say that nontangibles such as humor, prayer, attitude, the arts, intentional interaction with nature, and satisfying work all influence the positive functioning of the mind.

Monitoring. The functioning of both the conscious and unconscious mind is so automatic we tend to ignore it and its effects, or we assume that we can do little to manage it better or that such monitoring is too difficult. All these reactions contribute to mental unfitness. We can do better than this, and anyone who pursues a fitness quest *must* do so. It is not difficult to improve our skills in monitoring our rational and non-rational functioning. The key, of course, is to decide this is important, and then learn how to do it. I will suggest a few simple ways to become more aware of your own thinking, and I encourage you to develop these skills if you haven't already.

If you've ever taken time to do more than fix your hair or shave in front of a mirror, you may have learned how valuable it is to check out what happens when you have different facial expressions and different postures. Notice what happens as you watch yourself think about your reflected image. As you become conscious of what is going on in your mind, begin to think about your thinking, then about why you are thinking like this, and then about what happens when you intentionally change your thinking while watching in the mirror. For example, choose to frown, then smile, and note accompanying feelings and thoughts, and how you are thinking about this process. Children do this and thereby learn about self-consciousness.

You have probably done something like this before on occasion, but you may not have recognized what an important growth and fitness tool a mirror can be. You may have practiced different poses or practiced preaching in front of a mirror. Now you need to develop this skill as part of mental fitness.

Journaling. Your own handwriting on the pages of a personal journal (handwriting reveals more than doing this on a computer) gives you similar feedback about your thinking. This experience, however, is in terms of ideas and lived-experience rather than images and bodily movements. This means you can open yourself to the Think-2 level to allow bursts of insight ("Aha!") about how you are thinking, and how to improve it. Journaling also encourages the Think-3 level, which means you examine your behavior and thinking carefully, not in a critical, guilty sense, but rather as a way to appreciate what goes on in your mind. After savoring your responses to writing your thoughts (about whatever you choose to think about), you can begin to direct your thinking into imaginative and creative channels ("I wonder what would happen if I . . ."). Then tell yourself how much you enjoy God's remarkable gift of thought and awareness. Even if you don't like to write and don't like to observe yourself, you will probably find these exercises useful. Do some thinking and writing about your feminine and masculine characteristics and feelings. Write yourself a love letter. Note what you are proud of and worried about in yourself.

You may find it useful to have a checklist of items to cover each time you journal, or to cover occasionally in such writing. Noting unusual experiences and what these taught you; listing negative and positive experiences and why they were categorized as such; noting flashbacks and what triggers them; celebrating relationships; listing fears, hopes, and such—you can learn from recording all these things.

Feedback. Interpersonal feedback on how other people see and experience you (friends or enemies) offers insights about yourself that you cannot provide. Regardless of whether you like or believe the person giving the feedback, it is usually useful to process it by mirror and journal.

Decision making. We make thousands of decisions every day—most of them unconsciously. Some of these decisions are relatively minor, but others are major. Apparently we make most decisions reasonably well. This is one of the most important mental activities we do, so it is worthy of review. In fact, you may be making some decisions regarding your fitness quest right now. Decision making is a special way you can monitor mental fitness.

For example, if you are making, or have recently made a decision to begin or expand your fitness quest, take some time to think how you are making this decision. Are you making it in the same way that you usually make important decisions? How did you begin this decision? Did you gather data before making it? Did you simply feel that body-mind-spirit fitness is a good idea, and then decide to begin now? What was the determining factor in your decision? Do you approve of the way you make decisions?

Decision making is crucial to fitness. For at the beginning of a fitness quest you must make many conscious decisions, such as: what to eat and what not to eat; when to exercise and when to postpone it; whether to drink a glass of water or a glass of soda; whether or not to change your daily spiritual regimen. Even when you are experiencing the benefits of increasing fitness, you will be making decisions about continuing your fitness program, changing it, how to use the extra energy and strength you derive. On a bad day when you don't feel like doing what it takes to become or stay fit, you can learn from watching yourself make decisions about such feelings.

A major step in mental fitness is developing the ability to sort through the questions about and distractions to the priorities of a simple fitness regimen, and then just do it, without second-guessing or hassling yourself. This is tough-minded fitness: making simple, clear decisions and doing them. Warren Bennis, who has studied successful corporate CEOs, observed that one of their strongest attributes was giving themselves permission to make major decisions, and then let them be decisions. Mental fitness comes from making fit decisions, and fit decisions are a product of mental fitness.

The four laws of good decision making are:

1. Give yourself permission to make all necessary decisions—no outside permission needed.

2. Recognize that decisions are for effectiveness, not for approval.
3. Remember that if one decision doesn't work, you can make another.
4. Let a decision be a decision.

The best way out of double-binds, anxieties, confusion, and pain and into peace and confidence is to make decisions. Watch yourself do this better and better . . . it comes with fitness.

MENTAL FITNESS AND THE ABCS

"A" STANDS FOR AWARENESS

WHAT DO I KNOW AND NEED
TO KNOW ABOUT MENTAL FITNESS?

The human mind has been explored for centuries through philosophy, theology, and rudimentary science. And though there have been many conjectures and theories about how the organic brain-heart-other organs function, actual physical research on these organs was long limited to autopsies and dissection of the lifeless brains of animals and human beings. With the development of computer technology, various types of digital scans, probes, and tests are generating enormous amounts of information about human organs and their individual and combined thinking. For those who wish to explore this exciting frontier, several authoritative books on this research are listed in the bibliography. It is not necessary to be highly informed about this research in order to be mentally fit, yet recent research and information can certainly enhance our fitness quest. Let your personal needs and curiosity guide your exploration of advanced information about the body. The mind's awareness, which is important to body-mind-spirit fitness, is noted in several chapters in this book. The simplest guiding principles needed for your fitness quest are: a healthy body-mind-spirit connection; the increasing ability to monitor both conscious and preconscious mental functioning; an openness to personal mental experience (sensate, intuitive, imaginative, experiential, and outside feedback); and a disciplined regimen for mental fitness. Such awareness has been called "mindfulness" in Buddhist teaching for hundreds of years and made popular recently by Jon Kabat-Zinn in his books, training events, and laboratory. "Mindfulness" is a good term, for it reminds us of the value of such self-monitoring. It means more than just noticing some of our thoughts; it also means paying attention to our thinking continually and letting such monitoring be a peace-inducing experience, along with a learning process.

Awareness is both a general and a focused mental process that enables us to concentrate on a particular subject, object, experience, or person. In a fitness quest we need regular times to focus on fitness— the total experience of fitness as well as bodily, mental, and spiritual fitness. Answering some focusing questions can help you bring the experience of fitness into consciousness. Ask yourself, What does fitness mean, in general and to me personally? What does general fitness feel like today? What is bodily fitness for me today? What is mental fitness for me today? What is spiritual fitness for me today? What is my goal in body-mind-spirit fitness? What do I believe God's purposes in fitness are for me today?

If you have been reading this book thoughtfully, you will have received enough basic information to begin your fitness quest. And you are encouraged to bring your own experience, insights, and continued examination of body-mind-spirit fitness to the quest. I urge you to work to become more aware of your mental processes and of the quest for mental fitness, without anxiety about your mental states or capabilities. For the awareness I suggest here is an open-ended and joyful exploration of personhood—personal and corporate—that is available to anyone with normal mental capacities. But if you have serious questions about your mental functioning, consult a certified pastoral counselor or some other mental health professional who will take your religious faith seriously.

"B" STANDS FOR BASICS

WHAT ARE BASIC RESOURCES
AND EXPERIENCES FOR MY FITNESS?

The basic factors listed here are a combination of resource and experience. I discuss them elsewhere as they are related to body and spirit. Therefore, their application to mental fitness can be generic and brief.

Attitude. By now you have noted an emphasis on this subject as it relates to body-mind-spirit fitness. Attitude is one's basic mindset regarding a significant subject or condition. Your attitude toward fitness is crucial to your openness to the message and experience of fitness, and to your willingness to develop the basic disciplines necessary for achieving this satisfying lifestyle.

The basic ingredients of a fitness attitude are an openness to the adventure of body-mind-spirit fitness, the commitment to do what is necessary to develop fitness, and a sincere understanding that body-mind-spirit fitness is good stewardship of the personhood God entrusted to our care and service.

Nutrition. The ingestion of food and fluids was discussed in chapter 5, in terms of bodily fitness, and that material is relevant for mental nutrition also. Healthy nutrition and hydration benefit the brain, and therefore the mind, just as poor nutrition and hydration handicap mental functioning.

Less is known about nutrition for the mind than about nutrition for the body. However, knowledge about mental nutrition is increasing rapidly, induced in part by the recent emphasis on effective mental functioning in technological and professional vocations. Amino acids, enzymes, and hormones transmitted and interacting in fluids of the brain require carbohydrates (for glucose, the brain's fuel), protein for building muscles, vitamins and minerals for facilitation of chemical signaling and connecting in the brain, and hydration for the fluid needed as the medium for these interactions.

Ingesting a healthy balance of ingredients from the Food Guide Pyramid (see chapter 5) appears to be beneficial for brain-mind functioning as well as bodily functioning. And just as overeating is detrimental to the body, there appears to be a similar correlation for the amount and type of information and instructions we take into our minds. We can overload our minds, as many of us have learned through the experience of mental exhaustion and even burnout. Equally true, of course, is that underuse or understimulation of the mind can make it sluggish, lazy, inefficient, and bored. The point here is that in a world of media bombardment, intense human interactions, and growing obligations for survival, we must learn to manage our mental functioning more carefully than was necessary for previous generations. Few of us have been taught how to do this, and each person's needs and capacities differ, so we must learn for ourselves and from healthy models.

Exercise. Have you thought much about mental exercise? Theories about it abound, along with research data, methods, and experience, but each of us must learn what exercises our minds in healthy ways. The problem here is lack of knowledge, for many of us know even less about our minds and how to manage them than we do about managing our bodies. Since we will not be fully fit if only our bodies and spirits are fit, we must learn enough about our minds to manage them in healthy ways.

Perhaps your life already includes healthy forms of mental exercise. If so, then your task will be to vary your activities so that your mental exercise doesn't become rote. If your life does not contain many activities that require your mind to process new ideas; memorize; imagine new possibilities; create different tools, resources, and experiences; examine old habits; solve problems; feel new feelings; prioritize obligations; play exciting games; explore mysteries; and develop new relationships, then you are not only missing some fine mental satisfactions, but you are unlikely to be using your mind at a fitness level or developing its potential. For an extended discussion of specific brain exercises, *Listening to the Body*, by Robert Masters and Jean Houston, is particularly helpful.

Now may be a good time to review the larger perspective on exercise of all kinds. For exercise is more than stimulating the system at intense levels; it is also learning to relax, pace the exercise, blend work and play, explore new possibilities. The human mind is capable of functioning at high intensity for long periods, but eventually it must slow down. Though it never ceases functioning as our muscles do (although they continue to repair themselves and continue nutritional cycles, even in sleep, of course), we know that the mind can function at different levels of intensity and that the mind needs to balance high intensity brain waves (high energy output) with lower intensity brain waves in order to stay healthy.

One of the major skills of mental fitness is learning how to function as conditions require, without turning up the intensity level higher than necessary. A corollary skill is learning how to be creative while relaxed. Together these skills constitute what is called "being cool" in street jargon. These skills usually require mental discipline and practice, because the normal response to danger, opportunity, or obligation is to turn up the intensity. Living at intense levels for long periods of time induces burnout, the exhaustion of physical, emotional, mental, and spiritual energy, which often leads to permanent damage. You can teach yourself to be cool under pressure by purposely placing yourself in stressful settings and then practicing staying relaxed and focused on the task at hand. We will return to this issue later.

There are at least three mental exercises that you can readily practice and expand:

1. *Decision making*. This was discussed earlier in the memo section, yet it merits being noted again here. When faced with the need for a

decision, the mind typically either chooses habitual responses, post-pones or avoids making a decision, or seeks an innovative outcome. It will do this automatically unless we make a conscious effort to select one of the options. The mental exercise, then, is the use of various mind functions to review options and pursue one possibility until it works or must be abandoned. When we do not load the decision-making process with unnecessary expectations, decision making can be stimulating without anxiety, very useful, and even fun. You can both practice decision making and become increasingly aware of making decisions by noticing how many decisions you make all day long, and how you do it. Then practice changing decisions and noting useful and unwanted consequences. For example, choose to be wise, thoughtful, and relaxed as you choose how you will handle your lunch hour today. Enjoy.

We are deciding things all the time. Consciously or unconsciously we are deciding what to do, how to think, what to feel (attitude), continually. The power of deciding can become more conscious and can be used more intentionally, until it literally becomes a discipline. We need not allow our minds to be dominated by habitual thoughts or unthinking reactions to what is happening, or by the influence of others. We get to choose—we can decide—what to think, when, and how. This is not automatic, of course. We must first become conscious of our thinking, then notice how we can take charge of it. Remarkable things begin to happen when we are no longer victims of our own thinking—when we decide how we are going to think.

Body-mind-spirit fitness begins with a decision to become the best that you can be. Conscious decision making is then developed into a discipline in which you listen intentionally to what is going on in your brain-heart-body and choose more consciously what you will do with the marvelous gift of thinking. It is not rigid, stoic, judgmental, nor strident; it is joyful use of God's gift of thought.

2. *Experimentation.* Try a new recipe. Research an interesting subject. Learn a new language and culture. Go on a total fast (in appropriate circumstances). Change careers. Develop a new friendship—intentionally. Read a kind of book that's unlike your usual reading. Explore a fresh sexual relationship with your primary intimate partner. Do a week-long silent retreat. Study a different religion carefully (or if this feels threatening, a different denomination). Begin art classes, dance classes, yoga. The list goes on and on, with joyful possibilities, as well as the possibility of disappointment. And then another decision will be useful.

3. *Development-Enhancement.* We all have potential, much like a great underground oil deposit. Countless writers have written of these

undeveloped human capacities. A major potential exists in our minds—
the part of ourselves we seldom use. According to the bicameral brain
theory, most people have a dominant brain hemisphere, which means
one-half of our potential dominates. If one hemisphere of our brain tends
to be structured, orderly, controlling, the other hemisphere is more
open, aesthetic, spontaneous. We can see this in our personalities. It follows that with one hemisphere dominant, the other is less influential,
thereby short-changing us of the nondominant characteristics and
capacities. We can develop those other capacities with some mental
efforts.

Here is an exercise that demonstrates these hidden capacities. On a
blank sheet of paper, carefully draw a human stick figure, with your
pencil in your nondominant hand. Do it slowly and carefully, noting
the internal feelings associated with this unusual activity. You will find
that it takes more effort and concentration to draw this way than if you
did it with your dominant hand. The point is that with some extra effort
and concentration we can develop new skills that can be valuable in our
lives and ministries. Furthermore, we will find the special satisfactions
that come in developing our God-given potentials.

Try this exercise again, with the pencil in your nondominant hand,
and this time with your eyes closed. Again notice your internal feelings.
But this time also notice what it is like to tap into our remarkable mental capacity to imagine and do new things. Imagination is the raw material of self-development. When we take time to imagine (to mentally
picture) a different possibility, and then do it, we open many new areas
of our personhood. Mental fitness includes opening new areas of our
personhood for development.

Emendation. This is our ability to assess what and how we are thinking. Emendation is a vital skill for those who want to live with healthy
ideas and healthy relationships. We can use this capacity to evaluate our
major, life-shaping concept and accompanying presumptions to begin
to identify some flawed ideas and therefore some distortions in our lives
and ministries. For none of us has all of the truth or absolute truth. We
each, however, have some truth, mixed in with our preconceptions,
biases, prejudices, naivete, and thinking habits. With maturity we can
sort through our mental habits and ideologies and reality test them.
And, of course, those of us who take religious faith seriously also intend
to add God's gift of spiritual discernment to this sorting process, lest
we be confined in our own groupthink.

After many years in pastoral ministry and doing pastoral counseling

I am still amazed at the human capacity for using denial, reaction formation, and narcissism to conjure belief systems from our own limited experience and perspectives, and then convince ourselves that these are absolute truth. Of course we deny that we are doing this by appealing to proof-texts in scripture and the non sequiturs of our distorted logic. It is a wise person (one who is mentally fit) who is willing to examine beliefs and presuppositions prayerfully and in dialogue with other thoughtful persons to test the reality in our beliefs and be open to new insights from each other and from God's Holy Spirit.

If you haven't done this for a while, do some sort of systematic review of your philosophy of life, your attitude, and the everyday beliefs that guide your life. Do this with thoughtful peers, with your spouse and family, and with a mentor, pastoral counselor, or spiritual director who is also open to honest review of ideologies.

In a constantly changing world, which we assume God still loves and rules, an effective pastor must be able to assist parishioners in sorting out eternal verities from passing fads. The book of Acts is a remarkable example of believers who were willing to address the reality of diversity, open themselves to dialogue and guidance from God's Holy Spirit, and then by consensus develop a radically different theology that became the foundation of enormous growth in the early church (read Acts 15 to review this startling process). Those leaders are still valuable models for spiritual leadership today.

A practical, everyday kind of change we can make in thinking is to eliminate artificial deadlines, either-or binds, compulsive habits, and worrying what other people will think about us. When we take our cues and habits from a disorderly, anxious society, we are likely to lose peace and confidence. Taking time to set priorities congruent with God's purposes and our calling will give us steadying reference points as we go through the day.

Energy Management. I will save major discussion of mental-spiritual energy for chapter 7 but will review here five points regarding mental energy. First, all energy is a unified, dynamic power that both guides and fuels all of life. Second, energy is information as well as power (note discussions of "L Energy," in Paul Pearsall's *The Heart's Code*, p. 54, and in other sources). Third, energy comes from outside ourselves as the direct power to act, or as fuel (food, oxygen, fluids) that our individual physical-mental-spiritual systems transform into vigor, action, and thought. Fourth, energy is synergetic, that is, it can be pooled and enhanced (supercharged) when people gather, focus their energy, and "turn each other on." Fifth, each of us is responsible for managing our individual energy systems and sharing the energy resources available in God's creation.

Personally, each of us can move toward mental fitness by nurturing and managing our minds more consciously. Energy is a remarkable and potent gift of life. Our stewardship of it is a major responsibility.

Learning. Another basic is the capacity to learn. How sad it is to see adults who are stuck at an immature level of knowledge and understanding. Knowledge, wisdom, insight, and common sense are the goals of intellectual learning, although these goals are subordinate to the more powerful internal agendas of survival, identity, and relationships. (These will be discussed in chapter 8.) But we should note that learning is usually for a purpose, conscious or preconscious. This is why the authors of the wisdom literature of the Old Testament urge the development of wisdom. Proverbs 4:5, 7 indicates the difference between knowledge and wisdom and encourages acquisition of both. The difference between the two is important, for knowledge is essentially the accumulation of facts, while wisdom is the understanding of how these facts fit into the real world and life together. Greco-Roman philosophers identified the concept of self-knowledge ("Know thyself," Plutarch), which was later amplified by Alexander Pope ("Know then thyself," in "Essay on Man"). More recently clinicians and psychotherapists emphasize the development of insight, which is the mental capacity to understand oneself and accept a responsible place in relationships.

Learning is a lofty, fascinating, and dynamic mental process. Limited space precludes full discussion here, but readers are encouraged to explore constantly the learning (mental growth) process. For fitness itself is a dynamic growth process that occurs through the assimilation of facts (knowledge), tradition (wisdom), and insight (self-understanding).

Discipline. The discipline theme continues throughout this book because it is crucial to body-mind-spirit fitness. Fitness does not occur automatically, as we have noted. We may be blessed with health, good genes, and social privileges, but these are not the same as body-mind-spirit fitness. The fitness we are exploring is the intentional positive stewardship of our personhood (body-mind-spirit) in which we develop whatever genes, health, and circumstances we have into being the best that we can be. This is a function of discipline.

Mental fitness requires mental discipline, because our minds have an enormous capacity to absorb and be attentive to whatever captures our attention, that is, to be distracted. As we noted above, maturity and wisdom come as we sort through all the mental stuff we have accumulated to find appropriate priorities. And when we find them, we must enact them through decision making and discipline, lest distractions and other agendas sabotage fitness.

Mental fitness requires self-awareness, simplicity, balance, and tough-mindedness. None of these is normal amid the turmoil, change, and distractions of contemporary living. They must be learned, practiced, and enjoyed if they are to become a real alternative to the excesses now considered normal.

Self-Awareness. An emphasis on mental self-awareness is appropriate here in terms of learning how to relax the mind. When the mind is chaotic and churning with ideas and stimulations, it is difficult to observe it or identify our mental processes. Moreover, when such over-stimulation and distress are present, physical tension and spiritual confusion occur. Biofeedback is a reliable method for relaxing the mind. There are several ways to do this—with a machine that indicates brain wave intensity through sound levels or visual monitor, with yogalike mental manipulations of bodily functions, and with mental imaging combined with slow, deep breathing. This latter method is demonstrated by Herbert Benson's "Relaxation Response" in his book by that name. Later in this book I will relate Benson's method to spiritual fitness through meditation.

Another kind of mind awareness comes through examining dreams. Dreams in the Old Testament were taken as literal revelations from God. Sigmund Freud regarded them as a window of the soul, and dream analysis was important in psychoanalysis for some years. A common clinical perspective now is to simply note persistent themes in dreams as indicators of major preconscious themes in a person's life. A dream is often regarded now as a remembered mental processing of recent life events, often coded in symbolic images and experiences. Dreams should not be overemphasized, only noted as one indicator of the mental processing of significant experiences. The Talmud said, "The dream is its own interpretation."

Yet another indicator of mental fitness is the mandala, a geometric design used in Buddhism and Hinduism as part of ritualistic meditation. Carl Jung used spontaneous drawings of a mandala daily for a period as a visual representation of his moods and preconscious concerns. Any kind of spontaneous drawing can be useful in raising preconscious concerns to consciousness. Reading about self-awareness and therapeutic drawing may be useful to those who find it of interest.

Exploring the Inner World, by Tolbert McCarroll, gives a brief overview of this and other such self-awareness exercises.

Simplicity. Simplicity is the second of the four requirements for mental fitness listed earlier. I have found an aphorism from ancient philosophy enlightening to my understanding of simplicity: "He is rich who knows he has enough." This quotation contains the secret of contentment, too, as does the apostle Paul's comment, "I have learned to be content with whatever I have" (Phil. 4:11). Simplicity is not a normal response to life in our consumer- and addiction-oriented society; it is a learned discipline, and well worth the effort. Imagine how much calmer your day will be when you think, "I will be content with being the best that I can be today." (A fine discussion of this subject can be found in Richard Foster's *Celebration of Discipline,* Dallas Willard's *The Spirit of the Disciplines,* and Will Schutz's *Profound Simplicity.*)

Balance and toughmindedness. Balance and toughmindedness are valuable in self-management for these are conscious aspects of mental fitness. Balance is a common dynamic in our biochemistry, but we need to assist this healthy tendency by noting excesses and deficiencies in our lives, by watching for opposites and balancing them. In a fitness quest we must sometimes upset a long-established balance in order to achieve a healthier one. Toughmindedness is an attitude and skill by which we insist on honesty with ourselves and others and by which we sort through hype, misinformation, and illusion to find reality.

Healing. Chapter 4, on healing, discusses the transformation from sickness to health. I will only mention healing briefly here as it pertains to mental fitness.

Mental illness, personality disorders, traumatic abuse, and addictions are commonly accepted concepts now—as long as they refer to someone else. Mental fitness, however, requires that we take an honest inventory of our mental state and capacities. *The Diagnostic and Statistical Manual of Mental Disorders,* fourth edition (*DSM-IV*) produced by the American Psychiatric Association, describes many mental disorders. And for those with clinical training any of these diagnoses suggests a treatment protocol. Pastors need at least a rudimentary knowledge of mental disorders, for we are expected to notice when parishioners need assistance with mental disorders. But we as clergy *must* be aware of our own mental condition, and be alert to early warning signals of impending disorders in ourselves. Remember that the term "disorder," when used with a clinical name, does not necessarily indicate a dysfunctional person. Most disorders are part of relatively normal living, but they do indicate that something mental is malfunctioning and needs attention, and probably healing of some kind.

Four disorders are common among pastors today: depression, sexual malfeasance, post-traumatic stress disorder, and substance abuse.

1. Depression is now common—not the chronic, debilitating type (major depressive disorder, or bipolar disorder) but the everyday variety exhibited by persons living with high levels of stress continuously. It is often called generalized anxiety disorder in *DSM-IV* terms. The role of pastor is no longer clear, respected, and satisfying for many clergy. Unrealistic expectations, role confusion, denominational turmoil, and theological uncertainties produce a continuous mild depression. This condition can be concealed easily in a pastoral lifestyle, but it drains energy, reduces effectiveness, and tends to influence others with a negative mood and spiritual malaise.

2. Sexual misconduct and distorted thinking may be part of an obsessive-compulsive disorder, an anxiety disorder, an addictive disorder, or just poor judgment. The results, however, are often disastrous. It is reassuring to see how many denominations and congregations are taking this disorder and malpractice seriously, by establishing codes of conduct for both clergy and laity.

3. What I call the clergy killer phenomenon is a prime cause of post-traumatic stress disorder. For when a pastor, usually with collateral damage to family and congregation, is attacked abusively, persistently, and without supportive recourse by parishoners or colleagues, this can be experienced as traumatic abuse. The results are painful and damaging no matter what the mental state of the pastor. But when it traumatizes a pastor, the typical symptoms of PTSD become evident: flashbacks of the trauma, avoidance behavior in an attempt to evade further pain, depression, inability to trust. Pastors who have been traumatized in this manner cannot be expected to function normally.

4. Substance abuse, usually alcohol, is the fourth disorder among clergy and is common in society as a whole. Alcohol is legal and readily available, it is no longer perceived as disgraceful for clergy to use, its use is easy to hide, and it provides quick numbing of internal stresses. No one knows how many clergy abuse alcohol. The percentage is probably less than in the general public, yet those of us who work with clergy clinically know that the number is significant and seems to be growing. There's a message in there somewhere.

Fortunately, it is no longer disgraceful for pastors to be in treatment for drinking problems, and honesty, openness, and deciding that a call to pastoral ministry is too important to be sabotaged by alcohol abuse (or any other substance abuse) have led many pastors to seek treatment. Many treatment centers can provide effective therapy. Body-mind-spirit fitness is a lifestyle that excludes substance abuse because its internal peace and its focus on health and mission make chemical manipulations unattractive.

It is not uncommon for clergy to suffer from mental disorders. This is true partly because so many more mental conditions are now categorized as abnormal and disordered. It is also true because of the extraordinary stresses and vulnerabilities of contemporary pastoral ministry. Our society is exhibiting all the symptoms of distress, abuse, and mental-spiritual confusion. Pastors are needed to point the way toward wholeness. We can do this effectively . . . if we have found it ourselves.

Openness. Early in my pastoral ministry, I found Carl Rogers's book *On Becoming a Person* helpful. In it he describes "the fully functioning person," which was his term for a mature, well-rounded, responsible adult. The three characteristics that mark such a person, he said, were openness to experience, existential living (living fully in each moment), and a trust in one's own organism to guide one's living. Though this is not a Christian stance, his concept of openness enlightened me. I had been reared to fear the outside world and anyone different from me and my culture. With such an attitude I was essentially closed to any influence that did not fit my perspective on life. Not only was I closed to outside influences, I was closed to new information about what was going on inside me, and to anything outside that did not fit my prejudices and doctrines. God used this concept of openness, along with an extensive study of the book of Acts, to help me understand that my life and ministry needed to be open to other persons, open to other ideas, and open to the newness of what God is doing in this world. This insight has made an enormous difference in my attitude and my practice of ministry. I commend this concept to you as part of mental fitness.

Celebration. This term means praise, rejoicing, respect, festivity, exuberance. These words sound exultant, emotional, euphoric. Yet what organized religion has tended to do with this vital part of worship and healthy living is to stultify it with ritual, formality, solemnity, and political correctness, thus limiting its liberating, healing, and healthful effects. Now, in an effort to restore the joyfulness of celebration, communities of faith are using correctives such as passionate music, dance, spontaneity, charismatic devotion, and even playfulness. There is a similar movement in mental health circles to use humor, playfulness, and passion to induce endorphins (peptide hormones that ameliorate pain and generate good feelings) and encourage relaxation and healing. Even street jargon encourages us to "lighten up," or "chill out," or "get a life!" The power-of-positive-thinking movement preaches celebration and possibility thinking as alternatives to stultifying solemnity and stodginess.

We all know the value of celebration in religion, but we worry about its excesses. Mental and spiritual fitness require this basic ingredient, and we can learn or relearn how to include it in healthful ways.

Service. Mission is important to mental fitness. This word sounds like a religious term, which, of course, it is. But it is also an important, dynamic factor in mental health and fitness. Forgetting ourselves and devoting our attention to serving the needs of others can be healing and healthful.

The mental fitness part of service lies in the outward direction of our attention, the turning away from narcissistic tendencies, and the openness to the needs of others and our ecology. The exercise of body, mind, and spirit in various forms of service are beneficial as both exercise and nutrition for the mind.

"C" STANDS FOR CONGRUENCY

This relational, interdependent, synergistic factor needs little attention here, for it will receive major attention in chapter 7, on spiritual fitness. Note, however, that the congruence factor in mental fitness is the necessity of managing your organic brain, its energies, and its penchant to spin off into imagination and illusion without the disciplines of simplicity, balance, and reality testing. Not only does mental power increase in compatible relationships, but such relationships help you manage your mental capacities and fitness. And the more intimate your relationships, the more you need to be aware of the fit and the blend between your mind and the minds of those to whom you are relating. For their fitness is as important, to them and to you, as your own is.

Note, too, that recent research shows that thought, energy, and memory are interactive among human beings and all living things. Physicists call this instantaneous exchange and interaction between all living things in our universe the "non-local" characteristic of life—its

ATTITUDE Thankfulness for my life Openness to God's purposes
DECISION MAKING Choosing instead of floundering Choosing peace, love, fitness
NURTURING Thinking good thoughts (Phil. 4:8) Caring for others and ecology
LEARNING Exercising mind and spirit Exploring God's purposes

Figure 1. The Body-Mind-Spirit Mental Code

"L-Force," or "Fifth Force." (This is discussed in Pearsall, *The Heart's Code*.) The point is that we do not have to work ourselves into exhaustion in order to experience the disciplines and the joys of body-mind-spirit fitness. For it is already occurring in much of nature, and we can participate as we open ourselves to the life-enhancing interaction going on all around us. Further, when we choose to care (love) instead of consume, act instead of worry, trust instead of criticize, then God's purposes are served. Our relationships and the unconscious sharing of all of life and energy in God's creation become an awesome and exciting frontier in body-mind-spirit fitness.

SUMMARY

In this chapter I have discussed some remarkable subjects, including cognition, the relationships between brain and heart and bodily organs, self-monitoring, our mental self-management, and again touched on the incredible interrelationships between all living things. As part of this summary you may find it useful to look at the "Mental Code" (figure 1), and then go back through this chapter and review the discussion of each of the factors in the code.

In the next chapter we will explore spiritual fitness. From the physical, to the mental, to the spiritual, body-mind-spirit fitness expands into living life to its fullest (John 10:10b).

7

Spiritual Fitness

> Build thee more stately temples, O my soul . . .
> *Oliver Wendell Holmes*

Spiritual fitness seems such a normal, expected aspect of a clergyperson's life and role. Clergy are locked into spirituality simply by being the identified spiritual and moral leaders in society. But some physicians do not observe good health practices in their personal lives; some lawyers lose a healthy legal-ethical perspective; some carpenters do not keep their homes in good repair. And some clergy are not fit spiritually. No human version of spirituality is so good that it cannot become better. Being the best that we can be includes getting better in spiritual fitness . . . no matter how good we are now.

In my ministry as pastor to pastors for both the Wisconsin Conference of Churches and the Minnesota Council of Churches, I did ecumenical surveys of the state of the clergy in those states. Approximately 22 percent of questionnaires returned reported a deterioration of personal spiritual health. This is a significant number for persons who are ordained to a life of pastoral ministry. An even more sobering reality is one that I discovered in twenty-five years of pastoral counseling with clergy and their families, namely, that some pastors are not even aware of their spiritual unfitness.

If you are spiritually fit, give thanks for this, and continue your spiritual fitness practices. If you are not, or are becoming aware that you may not be fit spiritually, let this chapter be a welcomed invitation to renew the practice of spiritual fitness.

Spiritual fitness is not an end in itself nor is it simply a professional obligation. It is part of the healthy, joyful lifestyle I call fitness. And, as

I have noted regarding bodily fitness and mental fitness, spiritual fitness is not full fitness unless body and mind are fit too. This is why we call this whole process body-mind-spirit fitness. And because such total fitness is a pilgrimage rather than a state of perfection, we call our intentional growth toward fitness a fitness quest.

No formal definition of spirituality will be offered in this book, except by inference from issues discussed. This is an encouragement for each reader to bring his or her own definition of spirituality and spiritual experience to this pilgrimage. For spirituality is a very personal, as well as communal, dynamic. No one can define it for your personal life. Yet we need each other and each other's experience if we are to understand spirituality in its broader perspectives. Isaiah 55:9 is always a guideline for trying to define and understand spirituality.

As I have noted, I believe that body-mind-spirit are different aspects of a full human personhood. The three are diverse yet similar. They are inextricably interrelated even while having unique functions. The variance in their material and immaterial properties does not preclude our bodies from having spiritual characteristics nor our spirits from having material manifestations.

The following discussion of spiritual fitness assumes demonstrable and ineffable connections of spirit with mind and body. Therefore what I have written about bodily fitness and mental fitness applies in some ways to spiritual fitness and should be kept in mind as you read the following discussion for an understanding of spiritual fitness. The anthropomorphic ideation here is not intended as a reductionistic understanding of spirit and spirituality. Rather, it is a sincere endeavor to try to understand and explain spiritual fitness in rational terms.

The ABCs schema will serve again to organize information and discussion about spiritual fitness. And as before, some memos concerning spirituality are first presented as foundation and guidelines for the ABCs.

MEMOS CONCERNING SPIRITUAL FITNESS

Realm of the Spirit. I assume that the spiritual realm includes both good and evil; that good is a function of God and therefore beneficent, and that evil is the opposite and countering force, which may be personified as Satan. God is good, life-giving, and loving, while Satan is evil, anti-life, and malevolent. God and Satan are spirit beings who can be represented by incarnations. And they can connect with and influence us, since we are embodied spirits. We have choice in allegiance to either one.

These two forces engage in a universal struggle recorded in the Bible and holy books of other religions. The struggle for control and supremacy is evident in all of creation, and most noticeably among and within human beings. We each, and together, must choose our allegiance, and reinforce that choice continually. Choosing to act according to God's purposes places us within the healing, healthful process God intends for the shalom (wholeness, peace, salvation) of humankind. In this context, body-mind-spirit fitness is choices and behavior that are receptive to and foster God's best intentions for each of us, and all of us together. Everyone must make this choice, and we make shared choices. Then we all live with the consequences of these choices. For example, if I choose body-mind-spirit fitness, I not only enjoy its benefits but contribute to the fitness of all of us together. The point here is that full fitness is a spiritual as well as a physical and mental choice, with benefits for all three, and corporate as well as personal benefits. Needless to say, choosing unfitness has opposite consequences, individually and for all. Choosing to be spiritually fit means choosing an allegiance. If our allegiance is to God, this requires spiritual disciplines oriented toward God's purposes. The benefits are body-mind-spirit fitness, and less vulnerability to the destructiveness of evil.

The spirit realm is not easily understood, especially because it is so different from the material world. Even though we participate in the spirit realm, our most conscious reference point is the body and the material world. Therefore, we have much to learn about this spirit realm, which seems so mysterious to us. *The Powers That Be*, by Walter Wink, and *A History of God*, by Karen Armstrong, offer exhaustive discussions of the spirit realm. (For a more evangelical perspective see *Confronting the Powers*, by C. Peter Wagner [Ventura, Calif: Regal Books, 1996]; *Power Encounters*, by David Powlison [Grand Rapids: Baker Books 1995].)

Imago Dei. "The image of God" is an ancient theological term that has several interpretations, from an imprint of the Creator on each person, to a crowning of human beings as the highest earthly form of creation, to a built-in capacity to know and love God and persons, to a communication factor in the God-person relationship that orients us toward God's purposes. This latter interpretation fits the understanding of spiritual fitness I discuss here.

Perhaps *imago Dei* is the name for a gene for spirituality. A report from the Human Genome Project notes a claim that a gene has been found that relates to the part of the brain that seems to hear God. We may need to observe this research for further insights regarding spirituality and religious proclivities.

Union-communion with God is a unique spiritual experience. The union part is both our inherent and our intentional contact and connection with God. The communion part is our openness to God's presence and purposes and the enjoyment of what is an eternal relationship that can enfold us to whatever depth we allow.

There is both an involuntary and voluntary dynamic here. God relates to us as part of the continuing creation process, whether we are open to this or not. We may, however, as part of our salvation and commitment to God's purposes "grow in grace" (2 Peter 3:18), as the apostle Peter terms it, or "grow up . . . into Christ" (Eph. 4:15) as the apostle Paul terms it. With the advent of Jesus we have a visual-corporeal union with God. And through the Holy Spirit we have direct and immediate communication with God.

It becomes apparent to anyone trying to be open to God's initiatives and purposes that a personal and corporate discipline is needed on our part for this to occur most fully. This is why spiritual fitness includes a disciplined, committed response to God that must be a daily and continuing orientation toward God's purposes. Such disciplined spiritual fitness is not just an intention, it is a lifestyle, a fitness quest that includes body-mind-spirit in the unity of our personhood. Therein lies one of the deepest joys of body-mind spirit fitness, for it is an alternative lifestyle. It accepts and participates in normal human life, but declines to be caught up in contemporary anxieties and fads. How good can it get!?

Designer Religion. The eternal longing of the creature for union-communion with its creator exhibits itself in unusual ways today, as it has throughout human history. After generations of standardized religion, two major trends are breaking this mold. One is happening inside organized religion as a "reinventing the church" movement. Another is outside the church in the emergence of cults, New Age religion, pagan (e.g., witch-warlock) communities, and eclectic breakout groups from traditional denominations and religions. Both of these general groupings are marked by the presence of "designers" of special versions or brands of religion. I call them "designers" because they are marked by glamour, hype, and ambition. In this media-consumer age many people are open to sales pitches, performances, and some form of comfortable, exciting religion. We've always had reformers and innovators in religion, of course, but part of the appeal of contemporary designers is that they sell excitement and comfort, using all the tools and trappings of the marketplace—videotapes, books, trinkets, symbols, and nearly anything that will remind us of them. Given our learned addiction to such methods, the appeal of traditional and mainline churches pales in comparison. But some people are still deeply attracted to traditional expressions of spirituality, and the clergy officiating in those churches must be sincerely competent, if traditional forms are to survive.

The point here is that there are so many changes, distractions, and gurus in religion today that a person on a sincere fitness quest must sort through a variety of possibilities to find the voice of God and a spiritual fitness that is worthy and provides satisfying values, experiences, and guidelines for living.

There is room in this mix for healthy agnosticism. This word does not mean atheism nor cynicism nor eclecticism. It is the British scientist Thomas Huxley's term for a healthy search for evidence before believing. Such a stance can go too far, of course, by never believing or committing to anything, or by questioning everything within the church. Yet a healthy part of spiritual fitness is openness to new leadings from God and the willingness to test possibilities in the crucible of experience and scripture. This is a day for prophets again. Nevertheless we have learned from history that there are usually more false prophets than authentic ones.

Sexuality and Spirituality. Theologians, writers of scripture, and even monastics have noted the relationship of human sexuality and spirituality. Yet this connection has frightened many believers and spiritual leaders over the centuries. Clearly sexuality is powerful. Like other gifts of God, it is open to distortion and excess. Yet few physical-mental-spiritual pleasures are as satisfying. Our present age continues the separation fallacy of equating sexuality with orgasm and physical attractiveness. So a healthy sexuality needs to integrate orgasm and attractiveness with the fullness of our sexuality. Beyond this must come a recognition of the connection between human sexuality and spirituality. Such recognition would bring sexual experience back into the health of union-communion with God as the context for all sexuality. This does not stultify sexual pleasure nor turn passion into a guilt trip. Rather, it liberates sexual feelings and expressions for the greatest delights and the deepest satisfactions. It ennobles sex without devitalizing it. Part of spiritual fitness is to enjoy healthy sexuality.

Intimacy is the relational aspect of sexuality. Procreation, pleasure, and intimacy constitute the sacred triad of human sexuality. Intimacy will be discussed as part of support systems and relationships later. Here we simply note the deep human need for "consistent, two-way emotional closeness, by agreement" (my definition of intimacy). For our lives begin with this foundation, and our identity and fulfillment are never complete without intimate relationships. (Note: For a fuller discussion of human intimacy, see chapter 18 of my book, *Ministry and Sexuality: Cases, Counseling and Care.*)

Transformation. Though transformation was discussed as part of wholeness and healing (chapter 4) and elsewhere in this book, we must note here that spirituality, and therefore spiritual fitness, is dynamic, lively, metamorphosing. We are spiritual beings whether we choose to allow our personal spirituality to be transforming or not, of course. Yet spiritual fitness occurs as we allow our spirits to participate fully in the spirituality God established in all of creation, with the highest form reserved for humankind, namely, union-communion with God.

The Sacred. Sacredness, holiness, reverence, awe are all part of the ineffableness of spirituality. These are nonconceptual elements of religion. Rudolph Otto gave us more specialized terms such as "numinous," "mysterium," "fascinans," and "mysterium tremendum" to help us break out of the inadequacy of popularized terms that had lost some of their power to move us. Whenever I want to experience fascination and awe with the mystery of God ("fascinans"), I turn to the dramatic vision of Isaiah (Isa. 6:1–8) or the metaphysical description of Jesus with God and as God in the beginning and then metamorphosing into Jesus the Christ coming to earth in visible form as the light and the word.

Since God is "wholly other" (Otto, Tillich, Barth, e.g.) and we are human, the gap between us is enormous without God's grace and revelations of "I AM-ness" (Ex. 3:14). Yet our need for God is a primary yearning so deep that it must be satisfied. Without a visible God we can define and control, we tend to create such a God. Voltaire, the French philosopher said, "If God did not exist, it would be necessary to invent him." But the very idea of inventing God sounds blasphemous, so we must deny we invent our God (or at least the anthropomorphic ideas of God), and use quotes and implications from scripture to justify what we have imagined as God. J. B. Phillips warned of this tendency in his book, *Your God Is Too Small.* More recently Donald McCullough has alerted us in his book *The Trivialization of God.* Yet we continue to invent and imagine God as what we want and need God to be, for we may be too frightened to let God be so big (mysterium tremendum), so powerful and overwhelming (numinous), and so far beyond our control, that we can only bow in awe (fascinans), ask for cleansing, and open ourselves to the God who is higher than anything we can create or even imagine. Part of spiritual fitness is becoming so strong in our union-communion relationship with God that we need not create idols.

We should not ignore the growing number of references and materials that explore the role of shamans in human history. Though this is a foreign and even distasteful term to many, studying shamans does tell us something about the ancient roots of religious leadership. Mircea Eliade's classic *Shamanism* restored this term to contemporary religious consciousness. Since then Paul Ricoeur, Joseph Campbell, Huston Smith, and Karen Armstrong, among others, have helped us understand the shaman's role. Surely all the attention spirituality is receiving outside of organized religion speaks of a great spiritual yearning emerging all over the world, in reaction to secularizing trends. As clergy, we should at least be aware of the long tradition of shamanism, which exists in various ethnic settings even today.

The Call. Our calling to be pastors is imbedded in spirituality, at least in its ideal form. Of course it is related to our bodies and minds, but when we consider this role, which purports to point people toward God's higher thoughts and higher ways, the spiritual aspect of our humanity must predominate.

For generations organized religion assumed a lot about the call to be a pastor and added all kinds of rituals, mental machinations, and trappings to the role. Today a simpler call to be a pastor and perhaps a prophet is receiving more attention. And many are asking useful questions about our assumptions. What is the call to be a pastor . . . really? Is this call generically different than the "vocation" God gives to each person and to all of us together? How does the professional role that now dominates our understanding relate to God's call to be a pastor? Can I be a pastor without all the professional accretions? Is a pastor a "leader" or a "pastor," or both. As geofamily and global ecology perspectives gain influence, is a new version of pastoring emerging, namely, pastoral ecologist? How can I relate to the now-common diversity in congregations in spite of my personal heritage and trained biases? What is becoming clearer is that being a pastor (focusing on the congregation's spiritual needs) is primary, and other roles are secondary.

From an original function as mystical prophet and healer to a present day role as "pastoral director" (H. Richard Niebuhr), we've come a long way. It will take a while to sort out God's call from human manipulations and idolatry. Yet we need not wait for a clear theology to emerge and for organized religion to reinvent the clergy role. In some ways we are back to the situation at the time of the book of the Acts of the Apostles. Of course we cannot recreate those conditions or pretend to enact the role of apostle. What can we do if we feel called by God to be a pastor, and this call is authenticated in spiritually healthy ways? I do not pretend to have the answers, and especially not *your* answer. I simply ask all of us together to recognize the poor fit between God's call to pastoral ministry today and the clergy role developed by organized religion.

While confusing and even frightening, this generation of pastors seems called beyond some of the present designer and administrative tinkering with the role, and beyond "back to the basics," to "waiting on the Lord." As I've pastored and worked with pastors over three generations now, I have been privileged to see trends. These are telling us much about contemporary spiritual leadership. Yet it seems apparent that we do not yet even know what God is doing or calling us to do as pastors. This is a time for patient trust in God's higher thoughts and higher ways and for opening ourselves to discernment when God's purposes and human need show us a clearer path. Body-mind-spirit fitness is the best preparation I know of for this new era.

THE ABC OUTLINE

Let us turn again now to the ABCs scheme in order to organize our thinking about spiritual fitness.

"A" STANDS FOR AWARENESS

WHAT DO I KNOW AND NEED
TO KNOW ABOUT SPIRITUAL FITNESS?

First of all we need to recognize that "now we see in a mirror, dimly" when it comes to spirituality (1 Cor. 13:12). We can conjecture, rationalize, and pontificate about spirituality, but without the spiritual gift of discernment we have only our own limited notions to guide us. When dealing with God's higher thoughts and higher ways (Isa. 55:9) we need spiritual disciplines that open us to God's thoughts and ways; we need the community of faith to critique and reinforce our understandings; and we need our own intentional fitness quest to make our spiritual experiences authentic and personal.

Traditional Christianity has long taught that spiritual awareness is based on God's revelation in Holy Scripture, the doctrines and creeds of the community of faith, and individual conscience. Some would add that we also need God's revelations through creation, along with dynamic, spiritually disciplined dialogue in the community of faith and dialogue with the non-Christian world, to inform our awareness of spirituality. There is a Christian version of spirituality. But we limit ourselves if we cannot put this version in a larger experience of spirituality that was present in God long before Christianity was developed.

Throughout this book I have urged you to bring your own traditions, theologies, and experience to this discussion of fitness, and that applies to spirituality and spiritual fitness. Awareness cannot be forced. You must open yourself to information and insights from outside yourself before your personal awareness can be expanded. This is an act of will, an attitude, a choice that will determine the scope of your personal spiritual fitness, and therefore your body-mind-spirit fitness.

"B" STANDS FOR BASICS

WHAT ARE BASIC RESOURCES AND EXPERIENCES FOR SPIRITUAL FITNESS?

From great theologians, artists, and philosophers, and from colleagues and my own experience I have identified the following as basics for spiritual fitness. I pray you will assemble and use a similar list of resources and experiences to focus and sustain your spiritual fitness regimen.

Serenity. In chapter 6, on mental fitness, simplicity was noted as a mental discipline. Serenity is a product of simplifying and focusing life. Serenity is an unusual word for our ears. It apparently had deep meaning for monastics, but it sounds more like blissful ignorance to us. Serenity, as used here, does not mean finally getting everything you want or escaping from normal obligations. It does not imply the Buddhist teaching to eliminate desire in one's life, although that is a fine idea. Serenity does not mean peace at any cost, or denial of reality, or passive trust that God will take care of everything for me. Rather, I use the term to mean contentment and trust in God's purposes. The more common term today is "shalom," which suggests peace, wholeness, completeness, salvation. So why not just use the word "shalom" here, instead of a quaint term like serenity? You can, of course, especially if shalom has retained all of its deep meanings for you, despite being something of a buzzword among clergy. If you prefer "shalom" as a focal word for deep peace, then use it. I prefer the somewhat musty word "serenity" because it seems fresher than the overused shalom.

The important thing is to find a word that means to you a combination of bodily relaxation, mental discipline, and spiritual peace. The concept of body-mind-spirit fitness should mean a deep sense of peace, the fullest experience of peace continually. Unfortunately, the term "fitness" today includes messages about trying harder, masochistic "discipline," and looking good. Yet the message of total fitness I am trying to convey begins with a deep foundation of serenity, a relaxed letting go, peaceful trust in God's purposes. Then come the disciplines that allow body, mind, and spirit to function healthfully. The serenity and the discipline together bring us into a union-communion with God whereby God's ways become our ways. Blending with God's purposes is serenity.

How is serenity achieved? I purposely framed this question in the American parlance of making something happen, instead of letting something happen. The posing of this question should be the starting place in considering this issue. When we realize that the call to fitness is likely to hook into our anxieties and drives, rather than our openness to God's purposes, we must reframe the question, perhaps like this: How is serenity most likely to become part of my life?

Books have been and are being written about this subject because so many people (inside and outside organized religion) are asking it. The bibliography offers several I have found helpful. For our brief discussion of serenity, I offer the guidelines that follow.

1. First answer the "why" question: Why do I want serenity . . . really?
2. Try saying some slogans and notice how they sound to you:
   "The peace of God, which surpasses all understanding. (Phil. 4:7)
   "Come to me, all you that are . . . carrying heavy burdens . . . (Matt. 11:28)
   "Wait for the Lord . . . (Is. 40:31; Psalm 27:14; 37:7)
   "Try wiser, not harder."
   "You can't light a candle in the storm."
   "Relax into your pain."
3. Do what you already know will help you relax/release/trust.
4. Intentionally learn some new ways to *open* yourself to inner peace.
5. When you find simple actions that assist you toward openness, do them regularly.

It is patently true that sloganeering and clever techniques do not produce inner peace. Yet a phrase from scripture, or a concise insight, or a wise aphorism can become a beacon, a light in the darkness, an anchor to hold us steady in storms. You may find it useful to compose your own mottos as guidelines for opening yourself to serenity. When you find ideas and exercises that help, put them together in a simple regimen that you can do regularly to induce or restore serenity.

Listed below are some simple methods that aid body and mind and spirit to relax, release, and trust.

This is an abbreviated version of Herbert Benson's "Relaxation Response."

- Sit comfortably upright (on a chair, or in a yoga position), or lie down, and ask your whole body to relax . . . completely. Wait until it relaxes as much as it can.

- Concentrate on breathing, then take slow, deep breaths, and enjoy this breathing.

- When comfortable with breathing, begin to count down from ten to one, focusing and picturing each number in your mind as you count down.

- When you arrive at the number one, picture it in your mind and hold that image from then on during the exercise.

- As you become more and more relaxed, keep the number one pictured in your mind and do not allow any other thought or mental image to stay in your mind.

- Enjoy the deep relaxation and peace for fifteen to twenty minutes, three times per day.

- Some people are able to reach deep relaxation quickly by simply getting into a comfortable posture, closing their eyes, and picturing the number one, or a relaxing scene.

Note that the use of deep breathing for relaxation and meditation is not the possession of one person or school of thought. Yoga, biofeedback, "Mindfulness," Ignatian spiritual disciplines, and many other strategies remind us of the value deep breathing has for body-mind-spirit fitness.

2. Another relaxation-release-trust type of exercise is known as "physical prayer," in which a bodily posture or slow movement is used

along with meditation and prayer. Choose from the following (some are adapted from Roberto Assagioli's comprehensive psychological system called "psychosynthesis"):

- **The prone cross.** Lie on your back on a flat surface with arms extended fully at a ninety-degree angle from your body, and your legs straight and spread slightly. With your eyes closed, relax your body and breathe deeply and slowly for a while. Use some focusing thoughts or mental images in response to your emotions or felt needs, or on general spiritual themes such as Jesus on the cross, yourself lying in a great cathedral, sitting outside Jerusalem on the Mount of Olives, floating down a peaceful river, flying gently high above a great river and then floating down to the water and merging with it. (Note: it is important to be comfortable and relaxed. If you have disabilities or physical difficulties you may want a pillow under your knees or other props to aid in comfort.)

- **Kneeling, traditional.** Kneel, on a kneeling bench or beside a supportive object, or without any support, hands clasped in a comfortable position, head bowed or turned to heaven. From this position you may read scripture, religious writings, say memorized poems or prayers, pray orginal prayers, or mix any of these. Let your body posture become part of your experience.

- **Kneeling muslim style.** Get on your knees, settle back on your haunches, then bend your torso till your head touches the floor. Put your hands flat on the floor beside your head. You may rock, raising your head upright and back to the floor, rhythmically if you wish, or stay down. Do meditations and prayers to fit your needs.

- **Heavenward.** Stand as tall as possible, then raise your arms toward heaven and hold them there as long as is comfortable, praying prayers of openness and receptivity to God. Pray with your mouth wide open, as if drinking in God and God's energies, if you wish. You may vary this by facing to the four directions of the compass.

- **Giving-receiving.** Stand as tall as possible, then turn toward each direction of the compass, reaching out your arms as if giving food or gifts or love to people, then bring your arms toward you as if to receive food or gifts or love from other people.

- **Embracing nature.** If you are a nature lover, you may simulate standing or sitting in your favorite sacred place or nature setting and imagine petting birds, caressing flowers or shrubs, talking to creatures, and so on.

- **Sacraments.** If you are without opportunity to participate in Holy Communion, you may find blessing in simulating receiving the elements or administering them, with liturgy, scripture, and prayers appropriate to your tradition. This cannot, of course, replace full participation in sharing of the sacraments in normal and regular settings.

- **Foot washing** (shared physical prayer). With other believers, do the traditional foot washing rituals, being very sensitive to each other's feet, and to being an agent of blessing as you do this. A shoulder-neck massage can have similar effects and may feel more acceptable.

Belief. It is obvious that participation in spiritual fitness does not occur in persons who do not believe in the spiritual dimension of human existence or the value of honing such participation into what we are calling spiritual fitness. Nevertheless, it is important to remind ourselves that such belief is a cornerstone of spiritual fitness, first, because we will not rise to the level of spiritual fitness if we do not believe in it to the level of commitment. Second, we understand that the act of believing is dynamic in that it enlivens the believer, and also that grace is imparted from God in response to such belief. Though we are primary participants in the process of all aspects of body-mind-spirit fitness, traditional theology recognizes that God and the community of faith are powerful partners, with God being primary to all of it. It is reassuring to understand that we are not in this fitness quest alone.

By belief, I mean what we have called attitude in bodily and mental fitness. We are painfully aware that there are hollow beliefs (as in lip service), hypocrisy, and incorrect beliefs. But the beliefs I include in spiritual fitness are the sincere, committed types of beliefs. Yet we know that we can be sincerely wrong and as zealous in our idolatries as in true beliefs. The attitude that is necessary for effective spiritual believing is mostly accounted for in the living of a spiritually fit believer's life. Nevertheless, there is little question that negative attitudes in bodily unfitness and mental unfitness influence spiritual attitudes negatively. Therefore diligence and discipline are a part of believing in spiritual fitness.

Sacraments, Liturgy, and Symbols. These are basic resources and experiences of spiritual fitness, and therefore of body-mind-spirit fitness. Sacramental-liturgical-symbolic aspects of spiritual fitness take different forms, and their function and efficacy are understood variously. Yet even the simplest forms of religious practices need more than normal, everyday living activities to highlight their distinctive role in healthy living, and to set them apart as a special and necessary transaction between God and humankind. Here again each person must bring the best of her or his tradition, theology, and experience to this subject.

Nurture. Is there a correlation between food for the body, food for the brain-mind, and food for the spirit? I believe there is, and that it is important not only to recognize the need for feeding our spirits but to actually do so in a healthfully disciplined way. The term "nurture" is used here to indicate a substantive difference between material nutrition and non-material nutrition. Nurture carries with it a sense of caring inspiration and training, something beyond the ingestion of food. This is important for the mind, as well as for the spirit. Aesthetics, ethics, reverence, respect, worship, and mission are all learned activities and behaviors that must be taught, modeled, and reinforced if they are to become part of a fitness regimen for the spirit. If this process is left to chance and natural instincts there is danger of only minimal nurture of the spirit, which severely limits possible levels of body mind spirit fitness.

Individuality and idiosyncrasy are necessary considerations in all body-mind-spirit fitness issues, including spirituality. Just as with the body and the mind, each of us, with appropriate help from others, must learn our own personal needs and capacities. Over the years we also learn what enhances and what erodes spiritual fitness. However, though there must be much latitude for individual participation in body-mind-spirit fitness, we are all "our brother's keeper" in two senses. First is our inherent responsibility to care for or at least not harm each other. Second is the interdependence factor, which means we must all live with the shared and cumulative consequences of each other's behavior. Thus we share responsibility for making or allowing spiritual nurture to take place through worship, caring, the arts, and ecological stewardship. And we are accountable to each other for paying the bills to make appropriate spiritual nurture occur. Though each of us has our own needs and tastes, we all share responsibility for healthy spiritual nurture, for the alternatives are not livable.

How each of us does spiritual nurture depends upon needs, traditions, awareness, and opportunity. We must take personal responsibility to fulfill the basic needs listed here, and which vary individually, or work together to develop more enriching nurture. We know the consequences of poor bodily nutrition, and we are learning that poor mental and spiritual nurture also produces negative consequences.

The bodily metaphor for nutrition includes the importance of hydration. This carries over into mental hydration because of the obvious organic needs of the brain. What is the spiritual correlate for the spirit? We can quickly make a connection between the water we drink and the water with which we are baptized. Are there other fluid needs and resources that correspond? We can suggest the oil of anointing, the wine or grape juice or water of the Eucharist, the water of ritual cleansing, the water of foot washing. The list goes on.

We can add other forms of nurture that apply especially to spiritual fitness, though these apply to bodily and mental nutrition-nurture in some way by definition. We note the significance and nurturing qualities of light (candles, fire) and its symbols. Incense and aromas have spiritual significance and nurturing capacities. Drama, music, dance, graphic arts, poetry and literature, storytelling, liturgy, worship, preaching, teaching, counseling, admonition, encouragement, caring . . . the list goes on and on, thanks be to God. Spiritual nurture comes from many sources and is abundantly available, though not always in expected and hoped-for ways. People who have lived under tyranny, deprivation, and martyrdom learned that spiritual nurture comes essentially from God, and therefore is never totally absent. We who live in privilege have different needs, vulnerabilities, and responsibilities for spiritual nurture. We must sort through our abundance and make disciplined choices about what is truly nurturing to our spirits, and how much and in what ways this is needed.

Exercise. What is exercise in the spiritual sense? Here again the bodily metaphor is both helpful and misleading. The obvious direct correlation includes the fact that our spirits need exercise. Yet we are not so sure what constitutes such exercise and how it enhances and fulfills body-mind-spirit fitness. It is clear, however, that loving care of others, stewardship of self and resources, and the struggle against sin and evil constitute exercise of the spirit. Intercessory prayer, pastoral counseling, liturgy, crisis calls, silence, teaching confirmation class—all are specific examples of what will be spiritual exercise for many. How many of these are necessary individually and corporately, and the realistic limits of spiritual fitness are not so apparent. These must be learned in healthful spiritual fitness regimens.

Again, however, there is the God-and-grace factor, the mystery of our createdness and God's purposes. It seems logical, given traditional theology, to assume that we cannot supply all the nurture or the exercise or the healing and growth necessary. We trust God for some of it. But we have learned that this is an active trust. Passivity in spirit induces vulnerabilities and sicknesses similar to those that occur in couch potatoes and those who abuse or neglect their bodies and minds. Spiritual fitness requires spiritual discipline as our part of such fitness.

Healing. In chapter 4 I discussed the basic resources and experiences of healing that apply here also. In the truest sense there is no healing without healing of the spirit. A growing number of physicians and psychotherapists are recognizing this. We clergy, who devote our lives to the spiritual dimension of human life, must participate more actively and definitively in the necessary partnership between all the helping professions. This may be a good time to reread chapter 4 on healing, and other literature on this vital subject.

Spiritual Disciplines. These were once the province of the high church traditions only. Now the full theological spectrum is studying, discussing, and participating in these disciplines with deep yearnings as well as curiosity. Evangelicals are developing their own versions, mainliners theirs, while monastics, mystics, spiritual directors, and liturgical clergy celebrate and teach theirs. Besides this interest in spiritual disciplines we have the contemporary influences of charismatics, New Agers, spiritual designers, as well as restorationists and revisionists. What a mix! Even the term "spiritual disciplines" is controversial, and many would disagree as to what qualifies as a spiritual discipline. How is a sincere believer to sort out what is valid and needed for personal and corporate spiritual fitness?

Again I ask you to bring your tradition, theology, and experience to this discussion. I simply offer a pyramid of spiritual disciplines that fits my theological tradition, ecumenical learnings, and personal experience (figure 2). I arrange this list in pyramidal form to continue the helpful model of the Food Guide Pyramid from the U.S. Department of Agriculture (without recommendations for daily portions, however).

Look at figure 2 and consider your reactions to it very consciously, for they will affect your understanding of the following discussion. Now, join me in thinking through the spiritual disciplines needed for the spiritual fitness part of body-mind-spirit fitness. You will note that this pyramid of disciplines combines insights from both theology and psychology. In my opinion and experience, theology and psychology are natural soulmates.

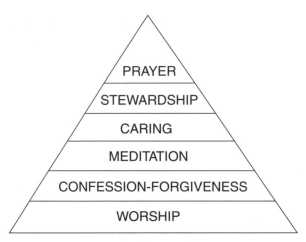

Figure 2. Spiritual Disciplines Pyramid

First, at the base of the pyramid is the spiritual discipline listed as foundational, namely, *worship.* Along with recognizing that all these disciplines are necessary and interrelated, and that each of us needs them in different amounts at different times, we can also assert that worship is primary.

Worship is union-communion with God. It is our awe, our reverence, our praise and love, our openness to God's thoughts and purposes. In a healthy worship experience we not only reverence God, we offer our questions, concerns, and stewardship. Worship is an attitude—an attitude that takes the reality of Creator-creature seriously, and responds positively. Worship is synergy—the pooled energy of a community of faith gathered to listen, confess, and feel beyond themselves, then to actively engage the outside world in dialogical living.

When I begin, continue, and close my day in an attitude of worship, my attitude and behavior are more likely to be marked by what Albert Schweitzer called "reverence for life," by the interpersonal respect Martin Buber noted in his "I-Thou" perspective, by joyful recognition of both limitations and potential, and by the satisfactions of being the best that God created me to be. Worship is not the only nor the simplest spiritual discipline. But for me it is foundational.

The ancient warning against idolatry is relevant here, for we still have a tendency to create our own gods. There is both an unconscious and conscious dynamic in contemporary idolatry. We create gods because we need them . . . desperately. Therefore it is natural to posit a god that meets our needs. We justify this, of course, by finding proof-texts in scripture, or by pious rationalizations. Our intentions are sincere but misguided. Since God is mysterious as well as present in some form, we have no clear picture to indicate the true God versus the one we create in our minds. When Moses tried to "see" God, he found a burning bush and a voice saying "I am." We need a God we can see and experience in some tangible way, as in Isaiah's vision in Isaiah chapter 6. Jesus testified that "whoever has seen me has seen the Father" (John 14:9). This was fine for the disciples, but we are left with a problem similar to that of Moses. Therefore we try to create God out of what we know or imagine, instead of letting God simply be God, which would require us to worship a God infinitely different than the one we create to justify our behavior, fulfill our imaginings, and favor us above others. So often in scripture and church history we have examples of sincere believers who created their own version of God, and then had to sit in a cave, wrestle with a night angel, or be punished in exile. When we try to create God, it means we are about as unfit as we can be, spiritually. Yet this is one of our most natural sins. We are forewarned to worship the true God, and to do this fervently and frequently, but in spiritually disciplined ways. God's commands to worship do not require perfection, only obedience.

Spiritual "love," another part of worship, includes hazards similar to trying to worship a god of our own creating. For the love commanded in both Old and New Testaments is a love God helps us develop. The human vulnerabilities highlighted by our sincere attempts to create God, and to love as God commanded, remind us that it is as easy to be spiritually unfit as to be physically or mentally unfit. It is a tenuous venture to try to create body-mind-spirit fitness, or any other spiritual mission on love. For the love many of us produce is a mix of romanticism, idealism, and projection. It takes spiritual discipline to develop a spiritual love that is not simply a product of our personal experience. Body-mind-spirit fitness is our preparation for other spiritual gifts, missions, and expectations. Let us worship God in spirit and truth.

Confession-Forgiveness is the second layer of the spiritual disciplines pyramid. It follows and builds upon worship in lived ways, for it recognizes our human condition, then attempts to purge the sin and evil in our lives in order that God's purposes may guide daily life.

Confession is therapeutic psychology. Here we recognize our flawed and limited condition. But we also confess specific mistakes and sins that interfere seriously and cumulatively with personal and corporate spiritual-mental health. Not only is it good to confess, but it is also good to share corporate confession and listen to others' confession.

This is not voyeurism, or masochism, or judgmentalism—it is acceptance of needed cleansing and a synergistic understanding of shared responsibility for sin and evil.

Forgiveness is part of liberating theology. Human beings can only forgive partially, but we can open ourselves and participate in the awesome freedom that comes when we "let it go," when we literally pronounce absolution as agents of God's grace.

So often I have seen and felt the emotion-spiritual release that came to clients or parishioners as I guided them through the confession-forgiveness process. This is salvation writ large! I encourage you to review the discussion of the forgiveness formula in chapter 4. Then revise it for your own life and ministry, for it is one of the awesome resources for spiritual fitness.

Meditation is the next level of the pyramid. Since this is a much used and much abused term, we should clean it up and freshen it for personal and corporate use. We know it is an ancient and noble term for a dimension of union-communion with God and the rhythms of God's creation. But how can we meditate in a plastic, paved, anxious context? We know the answer, of course, for Jesus taught us, and fine spiritual directors are giving us guidelines again. Meditation, according to my theology, psychology, and experience is a private, peaceful, focused stream of consciousness directed toward God. In meditation, which is built upon and includes worship and confession-forgiveness, I listen for God's Spirit, I dialogue with God's Spirit, and I reflect on insights thus gained.

Time limits impose barriers in meditation; nonetheless, meditation can be brief, if the appropriate conditions are present. Since few of us can spend large blocks of time meditating, developing an almost ritualized process can help. Establish a regular time, place, posture, and mental preparation routine. *What* time and place and conditions can be nearly irrelevant so long as they are consistent. This is what spiritual discipline is all about.

Meditation feeds the soul by allowing us to sort out ideas and experiences, masticate them, and digest them with rumination. Resources and props are appropriate so long as they are not distracting. It is the losing of oneself in union-communion which nourishes most effectively.

Contemplation, adoration, beatific vision, resting in God, and such are names for other ingredients important to meditation. Using your own terminology is important, but your own experience is most important.

The most satisfying worship services I attend include periods of silence in which gathered worshipers have an opportunity to engage in meditation. This is like an appetizer or inducement to good digestion of the spiritual food provided in worship.

Caring is our popularized term for love. When the word "love" ceases to carry intended meanings, we use "caring," although this word is now so abused as to be suspect as a description of Christian love. Yet no other theological or psychological term has captured as much of the contemporary meaning of our altruistic and disciplined solicitude. So we place this term in the hierarchy of spiritual disciplines, for we must have a designation for the outreach and respect factor of interpersonal relationships in spiritual fitness. We could use the term "love" in this spiritual disciplines pyramid. But it is so thoroughly contaminated by popularized notions and misunderstood theology and psychology that I prefer the term "caring," in hopes that we may rethink the holy meaning of love for our times. Note related discussions of spiritual love earlier in this chapter under the themes of meditation and worship.

Caring is a function of the heart more than the brain. Recent research on the human heart is confirming biblical language that speaks of the heart as the source of love and caring, rather than the brain. It is the human brain, in all its magnificent rationality, that often gets us off the track in spiritual matters. For we can think ourselves into any state we want (rationalizing) and congratulate ourselves on the achievement. Our heart is more honest, more fair, more in tune with God's purposes, and thereby a more reliable source for spiritual caring.

Caring as a spiritual discipline is delicate and strong at the same time. For it is sensitive to the personhood of others while insisting that good be done. Since this is a common theme for sermons and pastoral teaching, I shall assume there is no need for further explanation there. However, I do have two concerns for incorporating this concept into spiritual disciplines and spiritual fitness.

The first concern relates to how deeply ingrained the Golden Rule is in our thinking. In my theological and clinical experience I find a grave distortion in the noble teaching "Do unto others as you would have them do unto you." Jesus' intent, it seems to me, is to promote responsible and sensitive caring for others. The distortion comes in our popularized interpretation of this aphorism to mean that whatever I like, I may assume others like. And what I appreciate having done to or for me is precisely what others should want also. This sounds like the kind of arrogance and oppression minorities have been trying desperately to help the dominant Anglo and male power structure understand. If this is our stance for ministry, we are in serious trouble in the area of sensitivity to ethnic, gender, and class concerns of parishioners. It seems to me that Jesus was extraordinarily adept at understanding the cultural diversity of those to whom he ministered and sensing what they needed for healing and growth. We must use disciplined and informed ways of caring if we expect to reach people in their real needs, rather than in what we think their needs should be. A worthy guideline for caring could be: "We haven't expressed love until we've expressed it in ways which mean love to the recipient." For it is the needs of the recipient, not the projection of our own needs and standards on the recipient, which is the object of ministry.

My second concern regarding caring as spiritual discipline is that appropriate self-care (healthy self-love) is often neglected among pastors because of the exaggerated expectations of parishioners. A pastor taking time for appropriate self-care may be criticized and may feel guilty about this. Actually, healthy self-care is a gift to the congregation as well as to the pastor and his or her intimates. The real issues, however, are whether or not the pastor actually knows what her or his needs are and how to meet them in ways appropriate to the pastoral setting. This applies to knowing and meeting the actual needs of the pastor's family as well. In many cases of malfeasance by pastors I have found that legitimate, unmet personal needs are a contributing factor.

These two concerns highlight the fact that caring (ministry) must be a two-way process if it is healthy. If the pastor only cares for others well and does not receive appropriate care from parishioners or support for his own self-care, the relationships are likely to be codependent and unhealthy. Caring is a noble spiritual discipline—when done appropriately (in body-mind-spirit fitness).

Stewardship is often an uncomfortable and distorted spiritual discipline. Pastors have to deal with this issue in congregations year after year. But the point here is that stewardship is a personal issue for each of us. Excuses, good intentions, and illusions aside, the spiritual discipline of stewardship simply means disciplined care of self and personal resources, along with the shared stewardship of a congregation and all of creation.

This personal stewardship begins with disciplined body-mind-spirit fitness. "Fitness is good stewardship" is a basic premise of this book (see chapter 1). As you review the issues raised concerning fitness in this book, I pray that you will remember that body-mind-spirit fitness is the bottom line in stewardship.

I call this a spiritual discipline because it is not the norm for so many clergy, yet it should be. And it is a spiritual discipline because it is the primary covenant between our Creator and ourselves. You are the only person to whom God gave primary responsibility for the stewardship of your body, mind, and spirit. All else in ministry thrives or founders on this principle. The shared stewardship of congregation and ecology follows in good order if our primary stewardship is developed into body-mind-spirit fitness.

Prayer is the most obvious of the spiritual disciplines, yet it is often a source of guilt and confusion. Traditions and habits regarding this important spiritual discipline differ. I simply ask you to review your understanding of prayer and consider whether your present practices of prayer lead to spiritual fitness.

In addition to your considerations of what this discipline is for you, let me add two of my concerns. The first is the place in which I have placed prayer in the hierarchical pyramid of the spiritual disciplines. It is at the top, which in this schema implies the least important of the disciplines. What I want this placement to mean, however, is that prayer can easily be misused in a clergyperson's life. Many assume that saying a prayer is an instant recourse in nearly any pastoral situation, public or personal. In some ways this is a safe assumption because it fits public assumptions regarding our role and has become a personal habit for many of us. So prayer as a first or only response to pastoral situation and personal needs is normal, and certainly not bad. However, I believe that prayer is not really prayer unless it has resulted from the other disciplines, or is reaching toward them.

Prayer, as you note in the pyramid, follows foundational worship, confession-forgiveness, meditation, caring, and stewardship. When we have done the other disciplines, we have prayed all the elements of prayer. Therefore, formal and habitual prayer is less important, for the point of praying has already been accomplished. When I begin and continue the day in an attitude of worship (not solemnity nor piousness), I am praying. When I confess and forgive, I am praying. When I meditate, I am praying. When I do caring ministries, I am praying. When I do stewardship, I am praying. And when these are done, my prayers can focus on the joys of thankfulness and praise and return me naturally to the beginning of it all, namely, worship.

I am not denigrating prayer here. Rather, I am celebrating prayer for what it is most truly—all of the spiritual disciplines combined. And it is not prayer in its fullest sense unless the other disciplines are being accomplished.

It can be shocking to realize how much we use prayer as a diversion, a surrogate for the other spiritual disciplines, and an attempted short-cut to spiritual fitness. When I hear pastors talk of how much time they spend in prayer, I say a prayer that they are not misusing prayer. The need for prayer is great and obvious. But less prayer is needed if the other spiritual disciplines are taken seriously. I find myself praying less than I did some years ago, not because I am less spiritual or have become lazy. I pray more prayers of thankfulness and worship now because I have come to realize how much the prayers I used to make had become a substitute for the other disciplines. I have learned that I cannot be spiritually fit unless I practice all the spiritual disciplines. You may have other experiences with spiritual disciplines. Yet I encourage you to review your practice of spiritual disciplines to see if this leads to spiritual fitness, and therefore contributes to body-mind-spirit fitness.

My second concern regards a misuse of prayer. This is the intermediation prayer in which we ask God to do things we should do for ourselves. This is a way we avoid accepting responsibility for our own thoughts and behavior. If we pray, "God make me more like Jesus," we are telling ourselves and God that we may be unwilling to do and think the things that make us more like Jesus. And if we pray, "Dear Jesus, make me lose weight and do more exercising," we are asking God to do our work. Such poorly worded prayers are a kind of code in which we are really trying to tell God what *we* want instead of remedying our unhealthy behavior. It is true that God's Holy Spirit understands and decodes our prayers before God. The danger in such miscoded prayers lies in the subliminal message we give ourselves, that God will really do for us what we do not want to do. Our miscoded prayers can be translated into healthy action on our part. For when we thank God for the guidance already available, and the grace already present, we are reminding ourselves that God has already done God's part. Now it is up to us to enjoy God's participation in our fitness by doing our part.

For the times and places when praying is not easy, and our normal clergy-type prayers do not fit our needs or moods, it is reassuring to remember the apostle Paul's teaching that God's Spirit even understands our anxious, confused, and unsettling murmurs as prayer (Rom. 8:26–27). Sometimes when I have such experiences I simply resort to silence as my prayer, or pray the psalms, or borrow the Lord's Prayer or Saint Francis's Prayer or the Serenity Prayer. Asking or letting others do our praying is of course legitimate, as is going on about our day in a spirit of worship, which becomes our prayer.

We know and preach the instant and continuous communication God offers through prayer. It's even faster and more reliable than e-mail. Yet it is such a great gift that we should remind ourselves, and our parishioners, that it can be misused and abused. Recognizing the discipline part of spiritual disciplines can aid us in doing our part, assured that God provides the rest that is needed for our spiritual fitness.

"C" STANDS FOR CONGRUENCY

WHAT ARE THE SYNERGISTIC RELATIONSHIPS OF SPIRITUAL FITNESS?

The congruency factor becomes more inclusive and yet simpler and simpler as spiritual fitness is added to body-mind-spirit fitness—the fitness quest. Now I can experience myself as a worthy, healthy, participating part of God, of the community of faith, indeed, of all creation. Thanks be to God!

SUMMARY

This discussion of spiritual fitness can be summarized as follows:

- A–Awareness: I open my heart and mind as widely as possible, recognizing that spirituality is not a simple context for my rational mind. I humbly note that God's ways are higher than my ways. And I accept my responsibility to develop spiritual fitness through disciplined and joyous practice of spiritual disciplines.

- B–Basics: I give thanks and remind myself that I can and must relax-release-trust in order to allow the spiritual dimension to override my bodily appetites, my mental anxieties and habits, and my theological certainties so that I may be open to God's dynamic grace and purposes. Then the spiritual disciplines become a more natural part of my life instead of forced add-ons.

- C–Congruency: The union-communion with God and creation, the intimacy and shared spiritual energy of human relationships now add synergy to my spiritual fitness.

By implication the subject of this chapter raises the question, Is there a theology of body-mind-spirit fitness? Yes. I am offering my theology of body-mind-spirit fitness throughout this book. I do not, however, feel a prerogative of this book is the presentation of a formal theology. In fact, such an effort would distract from what I see as a crucial part of body-mind-spirit fitness, namely, developing a personal theology of body-mind-spirit fitness—one that is critiqued in the community of faith and tempered in the real world God gave us, and that we are now re-creating. Part of each believer's spiritual fitness will derive from the discerned theology she or he develops in body-mind-spirit fitness.

Since spirituality and theology are so dear to all of us as clergy, I suggest now that as a valuable part of the summary of this chapter on spiritual fitness, you add your summary of key issues discussed here, or that should have been discussed.

8

Fitness as Fulfillment

> Fitness is good stewardship.

"He is rich who knows he has enough." This Chinese proverb applies also to body-mind-spirit fitness. For fitness is about fulfillment, not about getting everything we want. It's easy for people in a capitalist nation to lose sight of little pleasures and deep satisfactions when indulgence and consumerism seem so attractive and available. But body-mind-spirit fitness is about simplicity, serenity, and stewardship, which are not achieved by purchasing the latest gadget or owning the biggest house. It is not about whipping ourselves with anxious slogans such as "Make every moment count!" or "Live every moment as if it were your last!" For when we are in a fitness quest, we don't need guilt trips and competitions. Instead, we tune ourselves toward God's purposes, which include all the fun, excitement, and deep satisfactions we need. Even retuning our tastes toward the simple things allows us to savor small precious experiences again, instead of trying to satisfy ourselves with consumptions. There is no greater reward than being the best that I can be . . . under God.

WHAT IS THE POINT . . . REALLY . . . OF BODY-MIND-SPIRIT
FITNESS? WILL IT BE AS MUCH FUN AS THE FUN I THINK
I AM HAVING NOW?

In the previous chapters I have made the case for a realistic kind of fitness for pastors that includes body, mind, and spirit—our full personhood. I have presented only a brief summary of the enormous amount of research data, psychology, and theology now in print as an impetus for your experience of full fitness. I pray we are all becoming convinced that body-mind-spirit fitness is necessary if we are to function effectively as pastors in the contemporary world. Is this another name for fulfillment?

In my judgment and experience body-mind-spirit fitness is its own reward and justification. Yet I believe we must also connect our fitness with another powerful dynamic of human personhood, namely, our motivational system, for no good idea or regimen will succeed unless it generates a sense of personal fulfillment. From Freud, Piaget, Erikson, Maslow, and others, we have learned that a powerful conscious and unconscious system of drives, intuitions, genes, and learned behavior is the engine for our motivational system. The term "attitude" represents the visible and mostly conscious part of such motivation. It is, however, the unconscious and habitually ignored or denied aspects of motivation that we must understand and manage if body-mind-spirit fitness is to become an established way of life—a fitness quest. This is a depth dimension for fitness.

AGENDAS FOR HUMAN BEHAVIOR

Over my years of pastoring and pastoral counseling I have studied psychology, sociology, and theology for insights into why people think and act as they do—why I think and act as I do. Such insights are crucial for effective pastoring and pastoral counseling, as well as for personal well-being. No one has all the answers to the why question, but many have valuable insights. I have distilled the insights I find helpful into a simple diagrammatical construct of human motivations (figure 3). Even with its limitations, this model, along your own ideas, can provide valuable insights for your personal life and pastoring.

As we have all learned by now, motivation is pivotal in transforming any established way of thinking and lifestyle. By "agendas," as used in figure 3 and throughout this chapter, I mean our habitual way of thinking and living. This is the normal structure and range of our emotions and drives, which we have adapted for personal living. Each agenda has a guiding question. The guiding question of each agenda is not changeable, but how we manage each one is adaptable. Body-mind-spirit fitness is the healthiest possible management of these agendas. This model doesn't answer all questions about why people behave as they do. But it can add another level of understanding that will contribute to your fitness quest. In this model, the foundational category is at the

Figure 3. Agendas for Human Behavior

base. Movement occurs upward as a person is satisfied with his or her progress.

The survival agenda is the broad, deep base for all motivation. It is the most powerful of the three. The identity agenda is the next most powerful. And the relationship agenda is the most tenuous as well as the most idealized of the three in terms of the emotions that mark each agenda. We know fear is the most powerful of all human emotions, with pleasure, anger, love, sadness, and joy following as less powerful, though important and very influential. And we know that though thoughts can be separate from emotions, they are often in service to our emotions. For example, when I feel offended or violated, my rationality is likely to be engulfed by emotional reaction to the offense. Insight and mental discipline are required to override an automatic, vengeful response. Power, as used in this context, means the force of our emotions and the drivenness of our thoughts. (Note: though seemingly judgmental terms are used in this model [negative-positive; higher-lower], they are only intended to be descriptive.)

The emotions that drive these agendas are distinct, and each is uniquely identified with only one of the indicated agendas. Yet these emotions are operative in all of life, of course. The two emotions identified with each agenda act as negative and positive poles of a person's energy system. Just as electrical current can move between negative and positive poles, so the biochemical-spiritual energies named here as familiar emotions generate a movement of the energy-current devoted to each agenda.

If you recognize that you are feeling angry or feeling very loving and confident, for example, you can recognize that you are probably in the grip of the identity agenda. Take each of these emotions seriously when they feel dominant, for they reveal much of what is going on inside of you.

Recall from previous discussion that human emotions have their source in our hearts rather than in our brain. We use all of our cognitive faculties as we live our version of these agendas. Our heart provides the emotions, our brain the thoughts, and our other bodily parts signal both heart and brain about our physical state. Growth toward body-mind-spirit fitness occurs as the brain processes information and decides how to live out each agenda. The heart adds the feelings and judges the brain's decision in reference to our intuitions and integrity, and our sense of meanings. And our bodies provide the physical vehicle for our behavior, and the experiential feedback telling how we are affected by our behavior. The survival agenda is essentially about the safety and health of our bodies, although it includes the need for a thriving mind and spirit. The identity agenda is essentially about the mind and its machinations, while including body and spirit. The relationship agenda is essentially about the spirit and relationships. Each agenda is natural and flexible. Body-mind-spirit fitness is about managing all three in healthy ways and according to God's purposes.

We should note that other living creatures have these agendas, too, though not in the highly developed form characteristic of human beings. Human groupings and organizations, including a community of faith, also have these agendas and unique adaptations. When we achieve facility in seeing and understanding these agendas, we have a valuable resource for self and for pastoring.

Each of these three agendas has a dominant, focused intention. This is why they can be called "agendas." When one or both of the identifying emotions dominates, there will be one generic and driving question to which nearly all of a person's attention is attached. The question doesn't go away or become less dominant unless it is answered in ways that satisfy the agenda. For example, on the survival agenda the only issue that really matters is "Am I safe here, and will I survive?" If the question is answered adequately, in the experience of the host person (the one having this experience), that person will be free to move upward to the next agenda. It is important to note that no amount of cajoling, hype, scolding, or inducement will move a person above the survival agenda, for instance, unless the focused question is answered convincingly, or unless an illusion is created that is strong enough to deceive the host person into imagining a satisfactory answer.

In addition to the driving emotions and the focused question, each agenda is guided by a dominant law of behavior. This law, in some idiosyncratic form, will govern the host person's thinking and behavior. For example, on the identity agenda, the law of competition is dominant. The host person will tend to see other persons only as competitors or sources of affirmation or denigration, until the focusing question, "Who am I, and what difference do I make here?" is answered convincingly by a person, organization, or experience significant for this person.

None of the three agendas is good or bad in itself. These are essentially neutral, normal human agendas, personalized with the characteristics of the host person. However, a person determines how each agenda is lived and may choose, consciously or unconsciously, to make it good or bad, or shadings thereof.

Now we can examine each agenda and the relationships between them in preparation for applying the body-mind-spirit fitness regimen to these agendas in order to keep them healthy instead of pernicious.

The Survival Agenda

The most powerful agenda of human motivation is the survival agenda. This is the agenda we are born into, though the potential for the others is present. And this is the agenda we are in continually, unless we have answered the survival question adequately and are reinforcing one of the higher agendas. This is the fall-back agenda (the "default" agenda, in computer jargon). Sometimes all it takes is a perceived insult or rejection to push a person down from the identity agenda and into survival behavior. Even if we have risen to the more comfortable relationship agenda, it may take only a criticism to push a person down to the identity agenda, and likely on down to the survival agenda.

A person stuck on the survival agenda tends to see other people as either enemies (threat) or friends (safe), and every issue or decision as either-or. Conflict is a serious matter, even deadly, unless trustworthy negotiation takes place. The law of behavior on the survival agenda is the law of the jungle in some form: "kill or be killed" or "an eye for an eye, and a tooth for a tooth." There are kinder and gentler versions, such as: "the survival of the fittest" and "live and let live," but this is still the law of the jungle.

In the church and sophisticated society (academe, social clubs, politics, and such) the deadly encounters may be camouflaged with smiles, ingratiation, patronization, even compliments and piousness. Some people may deny or not even know they are on the survival agenda. Therefore, it is wise to recognize the characteristics of this agenda. For many the survival agenda takes the form of aggression or avoidance, or a confusing mix of the two. Such behaviors help us to recognize the dominance of the survival agenda.

In the distressful, highly anxious lives that are now so common, the fear component of the survival emotions is triggered often, or it becomes the stressed-out response to everything, until the sense of fear threatens to overwhelm. This is daily life for some people. Since fear is so powerful and unpleasant in intense forms, relief and comfort are sought desperately. Stress-reducers and coping mechanisms provide quick relief, and pleasurable experiences provide euphoria, numbness, or diversion. For the harried, the worried, or the miserable, alcohol, sex, chemical substances, sleep, food, and escapism in various forms off-set the pain of fear (anxiety, worry, confusion). A variety of addictions are available to the desperate or undisciplined. Unfit pastors are vulnerable to all of this.

The good news is that the survival agenda need not become so desperate, and survival and safety can be assured, at least temporarily. Total security (meaning guaranteed survival), however, is illusory or seldom possible in contemporary society. Since a major part of safety lies in how we perceive ourselves and our environment, we can learn to act in safer ways, raise our fear threshold, and become more trusting. Our theology is a major antidote to overwhelming fear, if it includes a gracious God and a formula for behavior that assures divine protection. Though it is difficult, some persons on a relatively mature survival agenda can even find dependable comfort in God's provision of eternal life, no matter what happens to us in this life. This is available to all (Rom. 8:31–39).

Preachers, you should be alert to the possibility that you may be in service to survival fears or coping behaviors when you prepare your sermon or preach it. And you should include realistic reassurances and discussion of relevant fears and pleasures sometimes in your sermons, for a significant number of listeners will be on a survival agenda (because of conflict, divorce, job loss, grief, serious illness, crisis, failure, addiction) as they listen. They will leave with needs unmet unless they hear a realistic message of reassurance or hope.

By now you have guessed that people on the survival agenda simply cannot hear, or afford to notice, any words, issues, or events that do not speak to their fear or pleasure seeking. A sermon about love will go over their heads, unless it is related to their specific fears or need for comforting pleasure. Yet, when people hear words, see persons or cues, or are reassured by believable authority figures that inspire a sense of safety, they are able to move up to the next higher agenda. But they will not move until such reassurance occurs or is simulated in illusions.

THE IDENTITY AGENDA

The identity agenda is powered by anger or love. Its law is the law of competition. Its focused question is, "Who am I, and what difference do I make?" On this agenda the dominant emotions are anger and love, which are polar opposites. Anger can occur on any agenda, but as the dominant emotion on this agenda it is triggered by anything that is perceived as a violation of personhood, such as criticism, personal attacks, shame, inducement of guilt, or the frustration of desires. Love in some form is felt, however, when affirmation, affection, compliments, recognition, and even attention are perceived.

Anger is common and usually regarded as negative. But it is a normal, even automatic human emotion. We are born with this emotion as an immediate response to anything we perceive as a violation of personhood or frustration of personal desires. In the human brain, the limbic system is the primary residence of this agenda. Here the midlevel of the brain produces major parts of personality, handles some memories, learns, and responds to other creatures in more calculated ways. This agenda is positive or negative in relationship to genes, personality characteristics, habits, and reinforced behaviors. If a person has experienced traumatic abuse, emotional deprivation, isolation, or had negative mentors, it is likely that the way he or she lives will be a malevolent or narcissistic version of this agenda. A subtle version of such negativity is the passive-aggressive type of behavior. This is essentially behavior from a person who wants to punish the person(s) perceived as the one who has violated personhood or frustrated desires.

On the other hand, if a person has experienced sincere love from significant persons, seen models of healthy love, and lived in trustworthy intimate relationships, it is likely that the way she or he lives will be a positive version of this agenda. There is a message here for religious education and preaching.

We tend to assume that love is common and understood. But love is complicated and powerful, in both its positive and negative versions. Note that the three lower human emotions (fear, pleasure, and anger) are automatic emotions. This means that we are born with them and have no choice as to whether or not they will be triggered by certain cues. But we do have choices as we mature in what we will allow to trigger our anger, and how we will handle anger.

The three higher emotions (love, sadness, and joy) are learned emotions. We are born with the potential for them, but not the actual behavioral version. Love is an oft-studied behavior (Howard Harlow, William Glasser, et al.), so we now know that love can be learned in a negative version as well as a positive version. William Glasser taught us to understand that many "delinquent" kids have learned a negative version of love because they grew up without feeling loved and had negative adult models. On the other hand, kids who grow up feeling loved and seeing healthy love modeled by significant adults and peers, are able to give and receive healthy love. This is another reason I am uncomfortable with pushing love as the solution to all problems, and the ideal for all behavior. For love does not mean the same thing to everyone. A person who grew up and lives in a dysfunctional family or community may not even know the positive version of love. Therefore, a command to be more loving is confusing, or is an encouragement to intensify their negative version of love's potential.

On the identity agenda the law of competition says that I have to win, to beat others in order to win affirmation in some form, or back off and yield to persons perceived as superior. On this agenda just as in the survival agenda, intentions can be masked with such behavior as smiles, ingenuous compliments, cleverness, and hypocrisy. Yet the law of win-lose competition, and the question of identity remain operant till modulated by believable affirmation. When this is received, a person can move up to the highest of the agendas, the relational agenda.

THE RELATIONSHIP AGENDA

In the relationship agenda the focused question is, "How can we relate more positively?" The law of behavior is a search for and celebration of synergy. The third and highest level of our brain, the neocortex, is the residence of this agenda. This level is unique to humankind, a processing and mentation area of the brain that can lift us beyond reaction and action to proaction, beyond survival and competition to healthy relationships. Yet empowering the neocortex requires mental discipline. Mental fitness is mandatory, for a deep conflict, a traumatic event, or even the accumulating little negative experiences of everyday life can push the unfit down to the struggles of lower agendas. The good news is that you can learn to answer the key questions of the lower agendas quickly and believably, so that you can spend much of your day—your life—on the relational agenda.

HOW BODY-MIND-SPIRIT FITNESS AFFECTS THE AGENDAS

Now we can combine body-mind-spirit fitness and the agendas of human behavior to indicate possibilities for how a fully fit person handles the three agendas.

THE SURVIVAL AGENDA AND BODY-MIND-SPIRIT FITNESS

Bodily Fitness. Bodily fitness complements the survival agenda because it is essentially a physical agenda. Fear and pleasure are bodily emotions, for the whole body reacts to fear cues and to pleasure and mental euphoria. Moreover a strong body provides a sense of physical confidence in the ability to defend against or attack an enemy. Our task in body-mind-spirit fitness is to team the mind and spirit with bodily fitness in order to think of physical fitness as good physical feelings and the ability to enjoy life in healthy ways. Further, with our sophisticated knowledge of disease and injury, we can connect physical fitness with survival in the presence of infection and accident rather than in the presence of enemy warriors, or vicious animals, or even oppressive tyrants.

Mental Fitness. Being mentally fit is a great asset in the survival agenda. A person who is mentally fit, alert, responsive, and innovative has confidence that even against big enemies and great odds he or she has an excellent chance to survive.

Spiritual Fitness. Spirituality is an unknown quality for many people. Therefore, many would not know whether or not they are spiritually fit, or how spiritual fitness would aid survival. Many who feel spiritually strong assert that spiritual fitness is actually God's strength resident in them through grace. Others believe that spiritual fitness includes confidence that survival on earth is not as important as eternal survival, which they associate with trust in God's mysterious but benevolent purposes. Yet another view suggests that if a person is spiritually strong this adds strength to both bodily and mental fitness—a kind of wholeness. Such integrated fitness makes survival more likely in any circumstance.

THE IDENTITY AGENDA AND
BODY-MIND-SPIRIT FITNESS

Bodily Fitness. Feeling fit physically, for either women or men, is a boost to a healthy ego. A sense of physical well-being makes it less likely that a person will have to compensate for bodily unfitness through extraordinary achievements or dramatic behavior.

Mental Fitness. Mental fitness presumes normal mental abilities; a fit mind need not be brilliant. Yet mental fitness includes an ability to think through the issues of this agenda—who am I, and what difference do I make—and come to a satisfying conclusion. It also includes an ability to receive and return love, even to initiate loving and caring relationships. This further enhances a sense of worth.

Spiritual Fitness. Spiritual fitness on the identity agenda is likely to mean identifying with an organized religion, or asserting spirituality in some other way that recognizes and validates the metaphysical aspect of humanity. Even those who deny spirituality are likely to have aesthetic, artistic, altruistic, or nature-loving activities in their lives that serve to feed the soul and thereby nurture identity.

THE RELATIONAL AGENDA AND
BODY-MIND-SPIRIT FITNESS

Bodily Fitness. Being physically fit usually makes relationships easier, particularly if attended by mental and spiritual fitness. Bodily fitness, in the body-mind-spirit fitness definition, includes self-control of the hormones, appetites, and behavior that could undermine healthy relationships. It also implies having more energy to share in relationships and in groups than an unfit person would have.

Mental Fitness. Mental fitness is particularly valuable for the relational agenda, for a healthy mind will be sensitive to other people's needs, know how to participate in healthy relationships, and be able to contribute rational skills and creativity to shared concerns and activities.

Spiritual Fitness. Spiritual fitness is more than "having religion"; it is an awareness of the interconnections of all things and all people. So a spiritually fit person or group is likely to generate and share a healthy metaphysical dimension. In healthy relationships this means the power of spirituality nurtures and supports the relationships, adding energy and confidence. If spirituality becomes parochial, resultant relationships may become codependent and feature groupthink. However, spiritually fit relationships are likely to express the best features of a group's belief system.

HOW THE AGENDAS AFFECT
BODY-MIND-SPIRIT FITNESS

After considering how body-mind-spirit fitness affects the three agendas, now think about how the agendas can affect fitness.

FITNESS AND THE SURVIVAL AGENDA

The survival agenda by definition is very powerful in human experience. When on a survival agenda either a person becomes physically fit in order to survive, or becoming physically fit brings a sense of well-being to survival, which nurtures the best motivations for surviving. Body-mind-spirit fitness makes the survival agenda clearer. We can see it for what it is—our all-out effort to survive. We can feel the strong emotions of fear and pleasure without being overwhelmed. And we are less likely to play these two emotions against each other. For example, body-mind-spirit fitness enables us to see what is happening when we use the pleasures of alcohol, eating, or sex to assuage powerful anxieties. We are more likely to understand when we become frightened of our pleasure-seeking and indulgences and either complicate our lives with guilt trips or become harshly judgmental about pleasure seeking. By seeing the value of the survival drive and the powerful emotions that are its engines, we can manage ourselves more thoughtfully. And we will be able to minister more calmly in harsh, threatening situations where people are on a survival agenda.

FITNESS AND THE IDENTITY AGENDA

The identity agenda is all about individuality and "doing my own thing." This agenda is sometimes out of control in our democratic, capitalistic America. We built a great nation on "rugged individualism" when there were plenty of frontiers. In this frame of mind we believe we must "take charge" and control our destiny, even while our heart is telling us to be cooperative and caring toward each other. We still struggle with how to live together so closely when we have to cooperate and care for each other in order to fulfill our personal and shared identities together. Now that we are so interdependent and have to deal with our diversity up close, we tend to slip back and forth between the identity agenda and the survival agenda. This complicates the natural competitiveness of the identity agenda with the harshness of the survival agenda.

But when body-mind-spirit fitness is operant, we are more likely to recognize our anger and love feelings and know how to manage them well, for we know the intention behind them. For example, when I am feeling excessively irritable and angry, I know that my personhood has been violated or is being frustrated. And when I feel enraged, I can understand that the survival agenda has been triggered and I am now both angry and terrified. This means that I must now find reassurance for both my identity question and my survival question. And when I am feeling loving, I can understand that normal hormones are in action here and that there are appropriate ways to fulfill their influence. I will also be more aware that on this agenda I am seeking and open to affirmation and attention, and willing to give these if my needs are met, too. And it is likely that with body-mind-spirit fitness operant, I will be able to postpone gratification of my identity needs until appropriate settings are available, and not have to resort to "killing" my competitors who are getting what they want. Nor will I have to slip into the survival agenda for instant gratifications to ease my disappointments.

Body-mind-spirit fitness will allow me to minister on the identity agenda more effectively. For I will be less tempted to scold and patronize as I understand the basic needs and emotions here and how to bless the situation.

FITNESS AND THE RELATIONSHIP AGENDA

Body-mind-spirit fitness lifts our relationships to higher levels. We understand that the harsh and uncomfortable emotions and potentials of the lower agendas are still present, even on this gentler agenda. Therefore, even more attention to these agendas and our body-mind-spirit fitness are required in relationships. Discipline and attitude are highly important, along with honoring the agendas of persons with whom we are involved. And the powerful shared ministries possible from this agenda will be more shaped by sensitivity to the feelings and needs of those to whom the group is ministering than when operating from the other agendas.

Intimacy is a special case here, in which all three agendas are potentially operant. Intimacy is consistent, intentional emotional closeness by agreement. In covenanted relationships there will be a sometimes volatile mix of fear-pleasure, anger-love, sadness-joy. For in intimate relationships (family, close friends, emergency groupings) there is an implied message of trust and caring, along with the vulnerabilities of "personality clashes." Emotions and needs are intensified by closeness.

Body-mind-spirit fitness does not guarantee you will avoid all these pitfalls, but it is likely to make us more sensitive to each other's needs and more disciplined in managing our own. And at its best, the relationship agenda, enhanced by full fitness, can generate ultimate joys. I hope that it is obvious by now that body-mind-spirit fitness enhances our intimacy (union-communion) with God, as well as our relationships with those to whom we relate closely in daily life.

BODY-MIND-SPIRIT FULFILLMENT

This model of human motivations and the generic functioning of the human brain-mind leads us to a useful definition of fulfillment. Fulfillment, in these terms, has three aspects: survival with a sense of being able to function safely in an unpredictable world; a personal identity that is appreciated and that is a disciplined stewardship of one's personhood; and relational skills along with the satisfactions of relating healthfully and synergistically for the benefit of all.

The fitness quest for body-mind-spirit becomes more and more worthwhile as we understand the depth, breadth, and height of its goals and its everyday achievements and pleasures and benefits. What could be more worthwhile than the fulfillment of personal potential by "being the best that you can be?" What could better satisfy the drives of the three agendas for human behavior?

Now when I plan a bodily fitness regimen, its worth is no longer limited to bodily health and feeling good. When I plan a mental fitness regimen, its value is no longer limited to intellectual maturity and achievement. When I plan a spiritual fitness regimen, its integrity is no longer limited to a denominational or cultural model. But, if these typical goals for one part of myself are no longer adequate goals, what is an integrated, worthy expectation for personal fulfillment and faithful stewardship of my call to pastoral ministry?

No one can answer this question for you. But we can all answer it together. The consequences of negative behavior are now uniting us in paying the bills and penalties for our indulgent, idolatrous lifestyles. Why not meet each other with worthwhile agendas, such as helping to bring the kingdom of God on earth; sharing a healthy stewardship of our ecology; and finding personal fulfillment through helping lead it?

One very specific project can be an enormous aid in moving each of us toward fulfillment of all these opportunities, a peer keepers support process. This can be any association of individuals who pledge to care for each other and hold each other accountable to be the best that we can be—individually and together. Sound familiar or inviting?

You probably know that the day of the loner is over in pastoring. In my years of doing psychotherapy and consultations with clergy, I noted that an early warning signal of personal and professional problems is behavior that isolates a pastor from sources of support and accountability. None of us is so good that we can be wholly fit and faithful stewards of our calling all alone. And even though we can make realistic protests that "we don't have time," "there are no other pastors nearby," "the other pastors do not reach out to me," or "who needs another meeting with obligations," this fact is demonstrable: pastors who are willing to reach out to each other and build trusting relationships are much less likely to commit malfeasance, become unfit, and miss opportunities for fulfillment.

There are many models for pastoral groupings, from professional ecumenical associations such as the Academy of Parish Clergy, to the local lectionary, coffee, or recreational groups. There is no universal or perfect model. We all have to adapt, because it is worthwhile. If there is a local clergy cluster, take the risk of inviting yourself. If there is none, start one. At the very least, find a competent mentor or confidant.

After observing and helping organize many such groups, I have learned to keep them simple, yet have these organizing guidelines:

1. Each member must covenant to meet regularly, except in emergencies.
2. The group should be small enough to relate closely and large enough to be synergistic (six to ten people works well).
3. Organization should be minimal—only enough to support worthwhile functioning.
4. The emphasis is on healthy sharing and supportive activities.
5. There is nothing to prove to each other, for each comes as herself/himself.
6. There are no right or wrong things to do, as long as there is consensus.
7. Confidentiality is crucial: no one tells anyone else's story outside the group.
8. The group holds each member accountable for responsible behavior and growth.

Your support group need not be clergy, of course. But it must be supportive in legitimate ways. It is risky to depend upon parishioners for dependable support.

A scan of recent research on clergy relationships (done by career development organizations such as Fuller Institute of Church Growth, H. B. London, the Barna Group, and others, including myself) produced some troubling statistics: 70 percent of clergy indicate that they have no close personal friend; 24 percent have been forced out of a congregation at least once; 75 percent indicate seeing negative effects of pastoring on their families; and more than one-third do not reach the fifth anniversary of their ordination. We can do better than this, but not all by ourselves.

Your personal fitness quest can be much more stimulating if there are partners sharing in it. Clergy support groups, even with their exigencies and complications, are bringing major sustenance and support to growing numbers of pastors around the country. You can be part of this movement. Body-mind-spirit fitness can become a way of life for pastors everywhere.

SUMMARY

One of the great benefits of pastoral fitness is its potential for modeling and teaching. Anyone who visits many congregations and denominational offices knows the malaise hovering over many. We have tried Band-Aids. Now we can get to the heart of the matter and learn that our basic stewardship and ministry is personal and corporate fitness. Health is as contagious as sickness!

Some fine new (and old) study programs that teach aspects of fitness for congregations are available. But few put all three aspects of human personhood (body, mind, and spirit) together for study and implementation. Nor do many deepen the perspective of their study programs by learning to manage the three agendas of human behavior. Perhaps someone will write such a body-mind-spirit curriculum for families, congregations, and communities. The benefits would be enormous.

9

Fitness for Congregations

> Do you not know that you are God's temple
> and that God's Spirit dwells in you? If anyone destroys
> God's temple, God will destroy that person.
> For God's temple is holy, and you are that temple.
> *1 Cor. 3:16–17*

The primary emphasis of this book is individual fitness. The point has been made, however, that authentic fitness not only requires a support system, it must include relationships of all kinds.

A religious congregation is a function of relationships—relationships with God, relationship between pastor and laity, relationships among parishioners, and relationships to the larger community. In fact, the most potent factor in congregational life is interpersonal relationships. We have become so interrelated and interdependent that our only choices are about how we will relate.

The theology and spiritual dynamics of all this relating have to do with positive and negative interactions with God's purposes. Yet such lofty domains and concepts are lived out in ordinary, everyday decisions and experiences. Our human task is to be the best that we can be—individually, and in community with one another.

Fitness, when applied to a congregation, has the same meaning as when applied to individuals, namely, "intentional, interactive wellness." Again, as with an individual quest for fitness, each of the three words in this brief definition are dynamically important. "Intentional" means attitude and discipline. "Interactive" means the shared and synergistic experience of the group. And "wellness" means knowing the difference between illness and wellness; openness to healing and transformation; and communal stewardship of wellness for God's purposes.

Can we apply the term "fitness" to congregations? Yes. In health and wholeness thinking it commonly refers to any living organism and may be applied logically to a living organization. Though it is becoming encumbered with notions of muscles and sweat, it still calls us to be the best that we can be, as individuals and as congregations.

"Fitness" is a dynamic term implying intentional movement toward positive accomplishments. Therefore it can become an enabling vision for any thinking organism. A community of faith is a living entity, with many of the characteristics and tendencies described in this book. The Bible and traditional spirituality conceive of a congregation and its individual participants as living beings, having a material presence (visible, tangible), mental capacities, and spiritual dynamics. The apostle Paul is most specific in calling the community of faith the "body of Christ" and individual believers the "temple of the Holy Spirit" (1 Cor. 6:19–20; 3:16–17).

Though this incarnational model is common in traditional theology, many have been distracted by systems theory, family models, business models, and even the military models. When we think carefully about the incarnational model (the congregation is the "body of Christ"), however, its relevance to fitness becomes apparent. Then we can discuss nutrition, exercise, hydration, thinking, feeling, discipline, and mission in ways relevant to a living body.

CONGREGATIONAL FITNESS AND THE ABCS

As in previous chapters, we can organize our thinking about congregational fitness by using the ABCs format.

"A" STANDS FOR AWARENESS

WHAT DO WE KNOW AND NEED TO KNOW
ABOUT CONGREGATIONAL AWARENESS
AND PRACTICE OF FITNESS?

1. A congregation is a living body-mind-spirit. This means it has needs, identity, vulnerabilities, and potentials similar to its individual human members.
2. A congregation is created as a function of God's purposes. Therefore it is marked by the *imago Dei*, spiritual gifts, and a mission higher than its own wants and needs.
3. As is true of God's other creations, a congregation is capable of

generation, regeneration, and transformation. These dynamics are crucial for healing, growth, and mission.

4. When a congregation becomes fit, its synergy empowers enlightened mission. When it is sick or disabled, it needs healing, support, and a realistic sense of limitations.

5. A congregation has an internal nurture and guidance system, including its brain, heart, nervous system, digestive system, and personal identity. These elements require continual monitoring, evaluation and management if fitness and growth are to be sustained. And these elements are provided by human beings governed by their own individual elements. Leadership for this congregational organism will be compatible with its internal functioning and its identity. Yet leadership must lead toward fulfilling its calling.

6. Attitude is crucial for functional fitness. A congregation's attitude includes its tradition, habits, sense of identity, and vision of its mission.

7. Since this organism is composed of many individual organisms, the congregation's fitness is a balance of the fitness and unfitness of individual members. Congregational fitness will be influenced most by the relative fitness or unfitness of key leaders.

8. God's purposes, as expressed in all of God's creation, will modify and eventually circumscribe the fitness of any congregation. This means that if it is unfit, it will suffer the fate of any other unfit organism in creation. And if it is fit it will blend efficiently with all of God's creation.

"B" STANDS FOR BASICS

WHAT ARE THE BASIC INGREDIENTS
AND RESOURCES FOR CONGREGATIONAL FITNESS?

(Remember that the congregation functions as one living organism.)

1. *Nurture.* A congregation needs food for its material self, its mental self, and its spiritual self. It can choose junk food or good food, too much or too little.

2. *Hydration.* Fluids are important for the body-mind-spirit of a congregation. Fluids such as water, wine, and oil are both literal and symbolic.

3. *Exercise.* Just as a human body becomes flabby and vulnerable without body-mind-spirit exercise, so does a congregation. Each active congregation chooses exercises specific to its needs and mission.

4. *Discipline.* A congregation needs discipline (commitment, regularity, and systematic practice of regimens that produce and sustain fitness) as surely as individual persons do. Discipline in a congregation is provided by its bylaws, denominational polity, theology, liturgy, programs, and the influence of the community in which it exists. The aggregate disciplines of a congregation are a function of the individual disciplines of congregants and those determined by congregational decisions and behavior.

5. *Worship.* This is the attitude and behavior of a congregation whose point of reference is reverence for God and obedience to God's revelations and purposes. Worship is the primary spiritual discipline, for it is the source, empowerment, and mission of a community of faith. The worship we are referring to in congregational fitness is not ritualistic and thoughtless. Rather, it is the efficacious expression of salvation. And it is the full commitment of the body-mind-spirit of the congregation and its individual members. Such worship includes celebration, praise, prayer, the sacraments, proclamation, teaching/study, caring, healing, stewardship, and mission.

"C" STANDS FOR CONGRUENCY

WHAT ARE THE PRIMARY RELATIONSHIPS OF CONGREGATIONAL FITNESS?

1. *Union-communion.* This is the mystical yet very real openness toward God in which communication and love flow back and forth between Creator and creature and between participants in the congregation. It is the basic, intentional ingredient of worship, both corporate and individual.

2. *Body-mind-spirit.* This is the recognized and intentional interrelationship of the physical aspects of a congregation (bodily presence, tangible activities, material resources), the mental aspects (communication, decision making, attitude), and the spiritual aspects (reverence, stewardship, caring, spiritual disciplines). This fitness integrity means external integrity—witnessing to salvation and modeling discipleship outside the congregation, as well as integrity of relationships within the congregation. And it means consistency between what we proclaim and what we practice.

3. *Caring connection.* This is the active intention of relating to each

other in respectful and supportive ways in a congregation. It also means being accountable to each other for individual sharing of responsibility for the fitness of the congregation and for repentance and recovery when harm is done or responsibilities are not fulfilled.

4. *Synergy.* This is the augmented energy and support that occur in a group when members are committed to one another's welfare and a common mission. Synergy can be positive or negative: unfitness is contagious, but so is fitness. Moreover, when a congregation becomes passionate in worship, caring, and mission, it is transformed from being ordinary to doing the extraordinary works of God. This does not mean giddy euphoria or irresponsible passion. Rather, it means parishioners helping to turn each other on to the power of God in their midst. Each parishioner will have a characteristic way of participating in such fitness, yet will adapt individuality to the interests of the group and the shared mission.

TEACHING FITNESS

The gospel of fitness is wonderful, good news about the basic human condition. And many of us know the basic information about body-mind-spirit fitness. But putting it into practice requires more than approval of a good idea. This book is a primer for understanding body-mind-spirit fitness and learning how to put it into practice. Becoming a fit congregation is also a more complicated process than approving a good idea. A congregation on a fitness quest will need some guidance for this worthy process. Many parishioners are capable of reading this book and translating it into a fitness program shared with other parishioners. But most parishioners will need information, guidance, encouragement, and a practice and support process in order to move toward fitness.

Guidance and support for body-mind-spirit fitness in a congregation can be accomplished in a variety of ways. It could begin with a fitness retreat for leaders, or anyone interested. If could begin with a reading, research, and journaling project by individuals and small groups, undergirded by a church lending library of fitness books and equipment. It could begin with a fitness fair or exposition in which the whole congregation gathers for a day to see demonstrations of physical, mental, and spiritual fitness along with displays of healthful nutrition and exercise resources, with banners and posters and incentive products to encourage daily fitness, and including inspirational speakers and workshops. It could begin with a sermon series using the Bible as a text for body-mind-spirit fitness. And it could begin with a cluster of congregations, or a whole denomination. The concluding chapter in this book is a serious challenge to all pastors to join in leading any of these congregational fitness quests along with pursuing their own personal quest.

A standard way to develop worthwhile programs in a congregation is through the use of a curriculum for teaching small groups any appropriate subject. Body-mind-spirit fitness can be taught this way, using this book as a kind of text. It is beyond the purview of this book to offer a full fitness curriculum, but the following outline can be a starting place for a pastor or lay leaders who want to encourage body-mind-spirit fitness for their whole congregation. This is a simple, basic outline, which will need to be adapted to local situations. It can be taught in a variety of ways: by the pastor, by lay leaders, by relevant professionals such as physicians, nurses, pastoral counselors, spiritual directors.

The guiding principles for using this curriculum outline are simple and important: be positive; be practical; be honest about the pursuit of body-mind-spirit fitness and its disciplines; be supportive of all who wish to participate, no matter their level of competence or their limitations; relate this fitness quest to the mission of the congregation; provide continuing affirmation for individual and congregational fitness quests in any appropriate forms; offer the curriculum as an official congregational program.

A SIMPLE BODY-MIND-SPIRIT
FITNESS CURRICULUM

SESSION 1: WHAT IS BODY-MIND-SPIRIT FITNESS, AND WHY IS IT SO IMPORTANT?

(Distribute this fitness book, or Howard Clinebell's *Anchoring Your Well Being* [a leader's guide for using the book as a textbook is available from Nashville: Upper Room Books, 1997], or whatever resources are to be used as texts.)

Provide definitions of fitness, wholeness, health, and wellness. Discuss these topics.

Ask and answer the question, Why should our congregation be concerned about fitness?

Discuss why fitness must involve body, mind, and spirit in order to be effective.

Discuss the health and sickness statistics of our nation.

Identify the contextual features of our society that make fitness seem difficult.

Relate body-mind-spirit fitness to our spiritual heritage and mission.

Include testimonials of participants as to their own fitness quests, past or present.

SESSION 2: HEALING AS THE STARTING PLACE FOR BODY-MIND-SPIRIT FITNESS

(Show the healing resources common to your denomination: e.g., Bible, oil stock, stoles, prayerbook.)

Define and describe spiritual, mental, and physical illnesses and symptoms.

List the contemporary models of healing.

Discuss the various types of healing appropriate to your denomination.

Offer a model for a healing service, and do the service at least once.

SESSION 3: PHYSICAL FITNESS

(This is a good time to call in a physician, nurse, or fitness coach.)

Show diagrams of the human body and describe simple physical facts.

List and discuss the ABCs of physical fitness provided in this book.

Encourage participants to prepare a simple nutritional and exercise regimen to try.

Do some simple physical exercises and physical prayer in the class session.

Explore ways body-mind-spirit fitness can be useful for persons with physical disabilities.

Discuss stewardship of our bodies.

Discuss what physical fitness is for this congregation.

SESSION 4: MENTAL FITNESS

(This is a good time to call in a mental health professional.)

Show diagrams of the brain and offer simple information about its structure and function.

List and discuss the ABCs of mental fitness offered in this book.

Discuss some simple information about mental illnesses and mental dysfunction.

Provide some interesting mental exercises to demonstrate mental exercise and growth.

Discuss stewardship of the mind.

Discuss what mental fitness means for this congregation.

SESSION 5: SPIRITUAL FITNESS

(This is a good time to call in a competent spiritual director.)

Discuss contemporary understandings of spirituality.

Discuss what your denomination teaches about spiritual health.

List and discuss the ABCs of spiritual fitness in this book.

Have participants develop a simple daily regimen for spiritual fitness.

Discuss stewardship of the human spirit.

Discuss what spiritual fitness means for this congregation.

SESSION 6: BODY-MIND-SPIRIT FITNESS FOR INDIVIDUALS, FAMILIES, NEIGHBORHOODS

Discuss the realistic possibilities for this congregation to help unhappy persons, dysfunctional families, and distressed neighborhoods use body-mind-spirit fitness for healing and growth.

Develop a body-mind-spirit fitness plan for families to help make fitness a family project.

Explore ways body-mind-spirit fitness can be useful in your congregation's neighborhood.

Explore ways a congregation can use body-mind-spirit fitness for outreach and mission.

SESSION 7: WHAT THE GOSPEL OF FITNESS MEANS
TO THE CHURCH AND THE WORLD

This can be a wrap-up session with review, Q & A time, and "Where do we go from here?" discussion.

Develop a plan for making body-mind-spirit fitness a priority and lifestyle mandate for this congregation.

The gospel of fitness is an appropriate and vitally important theme for a congregation. It provides for salvation, healing, and mission in both traditional and contemporary ways. It is a focusing concept for the larger gospel of Jesus Christ. Jesus was a model of body-mind-spirit fitness from what we read of his simple diet, simple lifestyle, and spiritual discipline. Therefore our discipleship includes studying and modeling what made Jesus so effective in a ministry.

Developing a teaching curriculum for body-mind-spirit fitness in your congregation is a fine way to develop spiritual, mental, and physical health, which is highly effectively in preventing unhealthy conflict and promoting congregational growth. A healthy congregation is attractive in a sick world.

Conclusion

A Fitness Initiative
for Clergy

Health is as contagious as sickness.

What would happen if all, or nearly all, clergy in a congregation, community, denomination, nation, world, became wholly fit in body, mind, and spirit?

At first reading this sounds like a great idea but one unlikely to occur. Yet most great visions began with the inspiration of its inherent value, and wise leaders who made it happen. What if all of us who realize the vital importance of body-mind-spirit fitness decided to fan the flame of inspiration and develop a national clergy initiative?

A wave of popular consciousness-raising has already begun. Media and national leaders are citing statistics, with warnings of America's woeful lack of fitness and the enormous, largely unnecessary, costs this generates for each of us. Parishioners are becoming conscious of health and fitness issues, but many of them are unfit. Clergy are becoming conscious of health and fitness issues, but many of us are unfit. The popular expectation concerning clergy is that we will be advocates and models for the good and healthy things in life. Therefore we now have a choice: Will we help lead the fitness movement in the USA or will we be followers—or worst simply observers?

It is not necessary for pastors to lead and be at the forefront of everything, of course. And we don't have to lead the fitness movement all by ourselves. Yet we have a major responsibility to put fitness and health in a spiritual context for parishioners and our nation. First of all, we are obliged because health and fitness are spiritual issues. Second, we must put to rest the fads and misconceptions that are

167

confusing people about these issues. We don't have to become experts and tell parishioners what to do. But we can help keep priorities clear and help celebrate the good stewardship of body, mind, and spirit. Third, the statistics indicate that we pastors are as unhealthy and unfit as our parishioners. We need body-mind-spirit fitness for ourselves, and by getting on a fitness quest we can model the good stewardship of the body-mind-spirit fitness adventure. A healthy congregation and a healthy pastor—it doesn't get any better than this!

The U.S. Surgeon General, David Satcher, has reported that the government's Healthy People 2000 program, designed to help Americans achieve thirteen health objectives, has not been successful. In 1994, some 35 percent of us were overweight; in 1998, 54 percent of Americans were overweight. Being overweight is only one indicator of unfitness, of course. Yet the conclusion is that somehow the message of health and fitness must be taken to the grass roots of our nation. Seven professional organizations have joined to aid this project, including the American Heart Association, the American Cancer Society, and the American College of Sports Medicine. Pastors, who have direct contact with "the grass roots" every day, and who are designated leaders in most communities, have significant role suasion to use in this effort. It is compatible with what we do anyway in focusing attention on spirituality and spiritual well-being. Part of the message of the body-mind-spirit fitness initiative is that salvation, morality, and fitness are all part of the same wholeness package. It makes eminent sense for us to lead our congregations, denominations, and even our nation toward *total health and fitness, not just bodily health and fitness.*

I have been talking with religious and medical leaders about this subject for several years. Everyone agrees about its importance. Leaders in my denomination, the Presbyterian Church (U.S.A.), have been open to a fitness initiative. Several in other denominations seem cooperative. Some are holding conferences and writing books and articles about it. But the latest national statistics indicate only slight progress among our citizens, and in some statistics, we are going backward instead of toward better health and fitness. It seems to me that we have reached the second stage in a health and fitness revolution. The consciousness-raising is being done (stage 1). Now we need catalytic leaders to guide people into actual participation in the necessary changes in thinking and lifestyles (stage 2). Can you do anything to move your denomination toward a spiritual-mental-physical fitness initiative?

As I do seminars for pastors around the country, I find that we are in various states of knowledge and fitness. There will never be identical states or perfection among us, for each of us has a unique body and mind and spirit. And some of us have severe limitations, disabilities, and restraining medical conditions. Yet the good news about body-mind-spirit fitness is that this is not a competition, nor does everyone's body-mind-spirit fitness need to be identical. The goal is "to be the best that we can be" . . . together. What a joyful goal!

The point of urging national, ecumenical, and professional unity for this clergy fitness initiative is threefold: to encourage a collegiality not yet common among us; to emphasize that body-mind-spirit fitness is the best foundation for effective pastoring; and to develop an initiative for spiritual-mental-physical fitness that will guide our parishioners past the fads and gimmicks into wholeness (shalom).

My prayer is that we will learn and lead together.

APPENDIX A

Discussions about and descriptions of these exercises can be found on pages 90–91. Please consult with your physician before beginning any exercise program.

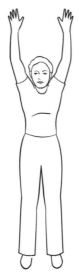

Alternative Stretching—
relaxing shoulders
(when no hanging bar is available)

Head—neck flexing

Torso—shoulder rotation

Windmill

Knee Bends

Erect Posture

*Flexing—
relaxing back/arms/shoulders*

Stretching—relaxing shoulders

Leg Stretches—
foot and ankle flexing

Lower Back Flexing—relaxation

Cat Stretches

Bun–run—rotating and flexing lower
back, hips, and shoulders

APPENDIX B

Fitness Worksheet

For your own convenience and reference, please fill out this worksheet thoughtfully. When you finish you will have a better understanding of the way you think about yourself and fitness. This worksheet will also serve as a reminder of your need for body-mind-spirit fitness, and your adventure on a fitness quest.

Your full name _____

Age_____ _____ Today's date_____

Height_____ Weight_____ Your Body Mass Index (BMI)_____
(To calculate BMI, multiply your weight in pounds by 703, then divide this number by your height in inches squared.)

Describe yourself physically and behaviorally as you would to someone who had never seen you.

_____

_____

_____

What is your definition of fitness?_____

_____

_____

The line represents your normal fitness. Along the time line, mark the peaks (above the line) and low points (below) in your personal fitness with dots. Each dot can represent a high or low point in your physical, mental, or spiritual fitness, or a combination. Connect the dots with a continuous line. Identify each dot by number and describe the event in the numbered blanks that follow the fitness time line. What does the line connecting highs or lows tell you?

```
B
I
R  -----------------------------------------    N
T                                               O
H                                               W
```

1. _____
   _____
2. _____
   _____
3. _____
   _____
4. _____
   _____
5. _____
   _____
6. _____
   _____

What do you do to keep your body fit now?

Nutrition _____
_____

Hydration (drinking water and other fluids) _____
_____

Exercise _____
_____

Work Activities _____
_____

Relaxation _____
_____

What do you do to keep your mind fit now?

Nutrition-Nurture _____

_____

Exercise _____

_____

Work Activities _____

_____

Relaxation _____

_____

What do you do to keep your spirit fit now?

Nurture _____

_____

Exercise _____

_____

Work (mission) _____

_____

Serenity _____

_____

What do you plan for participating in body-mind-spirit fitness (Your Fitness Quest)?

Body _____

_____

Mind _____

_____

Spirit _____

_____

Notes _____

_____

_____

APPENDIX C

Body-Mind-Spirit Fitness Quest

THE THREE-YEAR PLAN

No one can write someone else's plan for body-mind-spirit fitness and guarantee the outcome. Each of us must do this for ourselves . . . together. However, *Fit to Be a Pastor* contains the ingredients for a successful plan. The satisfaction and discipline in writing and living your fitness quest are yours. Yet all of us can use some assistance, so the following fitness proposal may be useful; feel free to revise it to suit your goal.

YEAR ONE

PREREQUISITES

1. Attitude—commitment to begin; openness to God's purposes
2. "Consociate"—a partner and support group
3. Physical, mental, and spiritual exams (use judgment, but don't neglect)
4. Equipment: basic nutritional, exercise, and service gear (keep it simple)
5. Basic library: start with this book, Koop's booklet, healthy recipes, and add to this collection as needed
6. Scale—yes, a scale (helps us stay honest, and celebrates physical fitness)
7. Journal—in which to record your fitness quest

A QUEST IN PROGRESS

1. Make this a year of exploration and experimentation as you seek to develop a workable regimen for body, mind, and spirit.
2. Start with fitness routines you know or want to try, and keep brief records of what works and doesn't work for you.

176

3. Develop a support plan of contacts and shared activities with consociate(s) and support group. This requires mutual, practical planning. Let it be exciting. Have spouse and family members join you with a fitness quest of their own in all possible ways.

4. You can start small or start big, or somewhere in between. Your body may have to adjust to new physical activity levels. But you should begin doing enough toward physical, mental, and spiritual fitness so that you feel positive results. For example, cutting the amount of food you eat, doing some regular flexing and exercises, and establishing a workable meditational process can begin immediately. You may want to find consultants to guide and answer questions if fitness is new to you, or if something occurs that worries you or you do not understand. Be careful of excesses.

5. Keep playfulness, variety, and celebration in your activities.

6. Don't be afraid of discipline. If this is new or different, start with small disciplines until you get the feel for making healthy decisions and sticking with them—whether you feel like it or not. Positive attitude and prayers of thankfulness help here. Remind yourself that disciplines are like brushing your teeth or studying for an exam. The payoff helps empower the discipline.

7. Set target dates for beginning and ending certain experiments.

8. Use caution in building "rewards" into your plans and activities, or at least make the rewards healthy ones. Remember that fitness is its own reward, and it is part of normal stewardship.

9. If you find physical, mental, and spiritual regimens that work for you, begin to establish them as regular habits and lifestyle now. You need not wait for one year to establish what works.

BASIC INGREDIENTS FOR YEAR ONE

1. Exercise regularly—daily flexing and warm-ups/cool-downs; isotonic and isometric exercises (increase repetitions for improvement and strength); at least one twenty-minute aerobic exercise or activity (walking briskly, jogging, swimming, racquetball, basketball) every other day; use stairs, not elevators; park farther from your destination; don't sit too long—get used to being physically active.

2. Eat less; eat smarter (better food, much less junk food and pop); hydrate; and weigh daily.

3. Give your body attention and care—massage, grooming, comfortable shoes and clothing.

4. Try fasting—in various forms and durations.
5. Try new, stimulating, learning activities as mental activities. Feed your mind with good ideas, and reinforce worthy mental work and relaxation.
6. Learn relaxation techniques and practice stress reduction.
7. Feed your soul with meditation, study, the arts, ecology, healthy relationships.
8. Review, evaluate, and invest in primary intimate relationships (family, spouse, close friends).
9. Reread this fitness book and related materials.
10. Begin to plan for year two by noting and reinforcing fitness practices and regimens that are effective and satisfying. Record everything relevant in your fitness journal.
11. Review your progress and plans with consociates, support group, and consultants.
12. Record and review sleep, recreation, work patterns—analyze for improvements.
13. Review your fitness patterns with intimates and discuss effects on them.
14. Share your fitness quest with parishioners as appropriate, and explore possibilities for developing a congregational (individual, clusters, and total membership) fitness quest.

YEAR TWO

1. Review journal entries for progress, patterns (negative and positive), gaps.
2. From what you learned in year one, lay out a physical regimen, a mental regimen, and a spiritual regimen that you can establish as a lifestyle.
3. Review all ingredients in the year-one plan regularly.
4. Optional possibilities for development (moving beyond level-one fitness): Take on one or more physical activities in which to develop special skills (strength training, tennis, wheel chair derby, arm wrestling, etc.); one or more mental development projects (memorizing, new books, leadership projects, etc.); one or more spiritual development projects (healing ministry, increased stewardship, work with Habitat for Humanity, etc.).
5. Make this a year to explore your limits and potentials, and record these carefully in your journal: physical limits and potentials; men-

tal limits and potentials, spiritual limits and potentials. Study your growth patterns in body-mind-spirit.
6. Become identified with your body-mind-spirit lifestyle. This becomes you and your stewardship, no matter the fads, temptations, and distractions. Let thankfulness and celebration undergird your fitness quest.

YEAR THREE

Principle One: Let spiritual disciplines undergird your life continually, while feeding your mind and heart and developing their potential, and while nourishing and exercising your body wisely.

Principle Two: Let lifestyle, journaling, relationships, and professional work and growth find comfortable yet responsible levels. Sustain these with both stimulation and relaxation.

Principle Three: Continue to explore and experiment responsibly.

Principle Four: Prepare fitness plans for transitions and emergencies.

Principle Five: Keep thankfulness and celebration as regular and spontaneous ingredients.

APPENDIX D

Body-Mind-Spirit Fitness Regimen Outline

DAILY-WEEKLY REGIMEN

BODY

Stretching—flexing movements (Do in early morning or at midday or evening.)

One aerobic exercise five days per week (Do warm-up before strenous exercise.) (Do 15 to 20 minutes per session.)

Eat less. (Down to one-half normal consumption)

Eat wisely. (Follow the Food Guide Pyramid.)

MIND

Prepare brief and realistic schedule for the day.

Do brief mental relaxation exercises throughout day. (Stretch slowly—especially shoulders, neck, and arms.) (Breathe deeply and slowly.)

Practice simplicity. (Keep lifestyle and decision making simple and relaxed.)

Keep a positive and open attitude.

Enjoy being your creative self.

Explore new/old ideas and activities.

SPIRIT

Develop a positive meditative exercise. (Do in early morning or at midday or evening.)

Do union-communion prayers throughout the day. (Savor relationships with God, persons, ecology.)

BIBLIOGRAPHY

This list of books is a small representation of the enormous body of literature relevant to body-mind-spirit fitness. Those marked with an asterisk have been particularly helpful to me. And those that I recommend for inclusion in a clergy body-mind-spirit fitness library have brief annotations attached. The health and fitness newsletter listed is simply the one I have found most useful. Web sites are too numerous to mention.

Armstrong, Karen. *A History of God: The Four Thousand-Year Quest of Judaism, Christianity, and Islam.* New York: Alfred A. Knopf, 1993.

*Ashbrook, James, and Carol Albright. *The Humanizing Brain: Where Religion and Neuroscience Meet.* Cleveland: Pilgrim Press, 1997.
    This book is another of the late Professor Ashbrook's masterful treatments of research on the human brain. He and Albright not only analyze current research but add the humanizing and theological insights that ground our understanding of our minds in both experience and spirituality. If only Ashbrook had survived to analyze the latest discoveries about the cognitive functioning of the human heart.

*Benson, Herbert, and Eileen M. Stuart. *The Wellness Book: The Comprehensive Guide to Maintaining Health and Treating Stress-Related Illness.* New York: Simon & Schuster, 1992.

Professor Benson was an early leader in translating the insights and traditions of Eastern psychology and medicine into the American idiom. He risked a great deal by promoting these insights and distilling them into a now-popularized exercise in relaxation and meditation, which is the core of his earlier book, *The Relaxation Response.* Now he, Eileen Stuart, and Joan Borysenko, among others at Harvard Medical School, are teaching the value of faith in medicine and healing.

Benson, Herbert. *The Relaxation Response.* New York: William Morrow and Co. Inc., 1975.

Borysenko, Joan. *Minding the Body, Mending the Mind.* Reading, Mass.: Addison-Wesley Publishing Co., 1987.

Buber, Martin. *I and Thou.* New York: Charles Scribner's Sons, 1970.

Cameron, Julia. *The Artist's Way: A Spiritual Path to Higher Creativity.* New York: Jeremy P. Tarcher Putnam, 1992.

Campbell, Peter A., and Edwin M. McMahon. *Bio-Spirituality: Focusing as a Way to Grow.* Chicago: Loyola Press, 1997.

Carrico, Mara, et al. *Yoga Journal's Yoga Basics: The Essential Beginner's Guide to Yoga for a Lifetime of Health and Fitness.* New York: Henry Holt & Co., 1997.

*Childre, Doc, and Howard Martin. *The HeartMath Solution.* San Francisco: HarperCollins, 1999.

*Clinebell, Howard. *Well Being: A Personal Plan for Exploring and Enriching the Seven Dimensions of Life: Mind, Body, Spirit, Love, Work, Play, the Earth.* San Francisco: HarperCollins, 1992.

Professor Clinebell is a pioneer in the wholeness-wellness movement in organized religion. This is only one of his writings on this subject. In it he provides a rich combination of human stories and insights, along with practical exercises and programs for applying his insights in everyday life. Best of all, he couches all this in a comfortable and yet prophetic spirituality where theology and psychology blend effortlessly.

———. *Anchoring Your Well Being: A Guide for Congregational Leaders.* Nashville: UpperRoom Books, 1997.

*Cooper, Kenneth H. *Faith-Based Fitness.* Nashville: Thomas Nelson Publishers, 1995.

Cooper, Robert K. *Health and Fitness Excellence: The Scientific Action Plan.* Boston: Houghton Mifflin Co., 1989.

Dossey, Larry. *Prayer Is Good Medicine: How to Reap Healing Benefits of Prayer.* San Francisco: HarperCollins, 1996.

Firshein, Richard. *The Neutraceutical Revolution.* New York: Penguin Books, 1998.

*Foster, Richard, J. *Celebration of Discipline.* San Francisco: Harper & Row, 1978.

For those who resist the idea of discipline, or worry about shallow piousness, this book will provide a deep spiritual understanding of discipleship, in a contemporary context. Foster makes spiritual disciplines seem so normal that we wonder why they have been lost to mainline theology and practice for so long. Along with his book on prayer, which may be the finest discussion of this mighty spiritual dynamic in contemporary literature, he gives freshness, practicality, and a sense of how discipleship can be a counterculture without being irrelevant. This book and Dallas Willard's are necessary reading for those who would pursue body-mind-spirit fitness.

*———. *Prayer*. San Francisco: Harper Collins, 1992.

Fox, Matthew. *Creation Spirituality: Liberating Gifts for the Peoples of the Earth*. San Francisco: Harper San Francisco, 1991.

———. *Original Blessing*. Santa Fe, N.M.: Bear & Company, 1983.

Fuhrman, Joel. *Fasting and Eating for Health: A Medical Doctor's Program for Conquering Disease*. New York: St. Martin's Press, 1995.

Gazzaniga, Michael S. *Mind Matters: How Mind and Brain Interact to Create Our Conscious Lives*. Boston: Houghton Mifflin Co., 1988.

Gleick, James. *Chaos: Making a New Science*. New York: Penguin Books, 1987.

Hall, Douglas John. *Thinking the Faith: Christian Theology in a North American Context*. Minneapolis: Augsburg Fortress, 1989.

Hillman, James. *The Soul's Code: In Search of Character and Calling*. New York: Warner Books, 1997.

*Holmes, Urban T. *Spirituality for Ministry*. San Francisco: Harper & Row, 1982.

Terry Holmes gave us what has become a classic resource in spirituality for clergy. His research and his lifelong devotion to teaching spirituality in pastoral ministry inform this book and make it one of the timeless guides to personal and professional devotion and meditation for pastors.

Kabat-Zinn, Jon. *Full Catastrophe Living: Using the Wisdom of Your Body and Mind to Face Stress, Pain*. New York: Dell Publishing Co., 1990.

Kelsey, Morton. *Healing and Christianity: A Classic Study*. Minneapolis: Augsburg Fortress, 1995.

*Koop, C. Everett. *On Your Way to Fitness*. Hanover, N.H.: C. Everett Koop Foundation, 1995.

This booklet is the most precise, straightforward, and informative piece of literature I know of for presenting basic information and guidance for physical fitness.

Kornfield, Margaret. *Cultivating Wholeness: A Guide to Care and Counseling in Faith Communities*. New York: Continuum, 1998.

This book is destined as a classic in contemporary care and counsel pastoring. It lifts the church's understanding of human experience, maladies, and potentials to nobler levels with elegant simplicity.

*Kybartas, Ray. *Fitness Is Religion*. New York: Simon & Schuster, 1997.

This book is a treasure of information, visual metaphors, and wisdom, all presented in the most appealing format I have seen for a book on fitness. It is also valuable for lifting our understanding of exercise and nutrition to the spiritual level. In ordinary, everyday terms Kybartas tells us that we dare not miss the joys of physical fitness.

MacNutt, Francis. *Healing.* Notre Dame, Ind.: Ave Maria Press, 1974.

Margen, Sheldon, et al. *The Wellness Encyclopedia of Food and Nutrition: How to Buy, Store, and Prepare Every Fresh Food.* Berkeley, Calif.: University of California Press, 1992.

*Masters, Robert, E.L. and Jean Houston. *Listening to the Body: The Psychophysical Way to Health and Awareness.* New York: Dell Publishing Co., 1978.

McCullough, Donald. *The Trivialization of God.* Colorado Springs: NavPress, 1995.

Merton, Thomas. *Contemplative Prayer.* Garden City, N.Y.: Image Books, 1971.

Moore, Thomas. *Care of the Soul: A Guide for Cultivating Depth and Sacredness in Everyday Life.* New York: HarperCollins, 1992.

Mottola, Anthony, ed. *The Spiritual Exercises of St. Ignatius.* Garden City, N.Y.: Image Books, 1964.

Nelson, James B. *Embodiment: An Approach to Sexuality and Christian Theology.* Minneapolis: Augsburg Publishing House, 1978.

*Nouwen, Henri. *The Wounded Healer: Ministry in Contemporary Society.* Garden City, N.Y.: Doubleday & Co., 1972.
    This is a classic presentation of the humanness of spiritual leaders. Its simplicity and wisdom must be read to be understood as the spiritual gem that it is—and then reread in order to let it impact any stereotypical practices in our pastoral ministries.

*Ornish, Dean. *Stress, Diet, and Your Heart.* New York: Penguin Books, 1984.
    Of all the books I have read on nutrition, exercise, and healthy self-management, this one makes the most sense. Dr. Ornish presents a holistic program for healing, health, and fitness, which includes nutrition, exercise, stress management, meditation, and support systems. This is physical-mental advice at its best from a medical professional.

*Pearsall, Paul. *The Heart's Code: Tapping the Wisdom and Power of Our Heart.* New York: Broadway Books, 1998.
    This book introduced me to the revolutionary insights of research on the human heart. Along with the HeartMath Institute's

materials and training, this book continues to open my eyes to understanding how much more than a pump the human heart is, and how powerful it is in comparison with the human brain. Body-mind-spirit fitness is not possible without understanding the development of heart-felt mental and spiritual insights.

Phillips, J.B. *Your God Is Too Small.* New York: The Macmillan Co., 1957.

Readers Digest Association, The. *Foods That Harm, Foods That Heal.* Pleasantville, N.Y.: Readers Digest Association, 1997.

―――. *The Good Health Fact Book.* Pleasantville, N.Y.: Readers Digest Association, 1992.

Rediger, G. Lloyd. *Clergy Killers: Guidance for Pastors and Congregations under Attack.* Louisville, Ky.: Westminster John Knox Press, 1997; Inver Grove Heights, MN: Logos Productions, Inc., 1997.

I must take the risk of recommending one of my own books simply because it presents the still-shocking dimension of traumatic abuse now engulfing about one-fourth of pastors in the United States. In my seminars on the "clergy killer phenomenon," I try to lead battered clergy on through their victimization into healing and a refreshing understanding of how valuable body-mind-spirit fitness is for managing the abusive types of conflict in congregations and in their personal lives.

―――. *Coping with Clergy Burnout.* Valley Forge, Pa.: Judson Press, 1982.

―――. *Ministry and Sexuality: Cases, Counseling and Care.* Minneapolis: Fortress Press, 1990.

Rice, Howard L. *Reformed Spirituality: An Introduction for Believers.* Louisville, Ky.: Westminister/John Knox Press, 1991.

Schutz, Will. *Profound Simplicity.* New York: Bantam Books, 1979.

Shamblin, Gwen. *The Weigh Down Diet.* New York: Doubleday, 1997.

*Tillich, Paul. *The Courage to Be.* New Haven, Conn.: Yale University Press, 1952.

Touchstone Books Staff. *Our Bodies, Ourselves for the New Century: A Book by & for Women.* New York: Simon & Schuster Trade, 1998.

This is the classic women's book on physical-mental awareness and liberation from stereotypes.

*Weil, Andrew. *Natural Health, Natural Medicine: A Comprehensive Manual for Wellness and Self-Care.* Boston: Houghton Mifflin Co., 1998.

————. *Spontaneous Healing: How to Discover and Enhance Your Body's Natural Ability to Maintain and Heal Itself.* New York: Alfred A. Knopf, 1995.

"Wellness Newsletter." School of Public Health, University of California at Berkeley. Rodney M. Friedman, Editor and Publisher.

*Willard, Dallas. *The Spirit of the Disciplines: Understanding How God Changes Lives.* San Francisco: HarperCollins, 1998.

*Wink, Walter. *The Powers That Be: Theology for a New Millennium.* New York: Doubleday, 1998.

    I can think of nothing that has had greater impact on my thinking and ministry than Walter Wink's trilogy on the spirit realm, which this book summarizes. This book adds insights and depth to the understanding and practice of spirituality that I have not found elsewhere. Because of this book I now have less fear of the spirit realm, and a greater appreciation for the power and complications of spiritual warfare. Yet it has also added deep and reverent dimensions to my experience of God and the mysterious realm of the spirit to which I am attached by my *imago Dei*.